WHAT CHURCHES OF CHRIST STAND FOR

THE ORIGIN, GROWTH, AND MESSAGE OF A NINETEENTH CENTURY RELIGIOUS MOVEMENT

By

WILLIAM ROBINSON, M.A., D.D., S.T.D.,

Formerly Principal of Overdale College, and Professor of Christian Doctrine in the Selly Oak Colleges, Birmingham; Professor of Christian Doctrine (Emeritus), School of Religion Butler University, Indianapolis, U.S.A. Member of the World Council of Churches.

BIRMINGHAM :
THE BEREAN PRESS
20, BRIGHTON ROAD, BALSALL HEATH
1959

CONTENTS

APPENDICES

First Published 1926 . . 10,000
Second Edition 1929 . . 2,000
Third Edition 1946 . . 5,000
Fourth Edition 1959 . . 3,000

PRINTED IN GREAT BRITAIN BY
THE BIRMINGHAM PRINTERS LTD., HILL STREET AND STATION STREET,
BIRMINGHAM, 5.

FOREWORD

THE Christian Church has ever needed to restate its faith in terms suited to each new age in which it has lived   And upon every movement within the Christian Church there is laid the same necessity of making itself intelligible to its own generation. Hence the first reason for the present work. Throughout I have had in mind many who may never have heard of the Churches of Christ in the sense in which the expression is used on the title page of this book, and others who, though they are acquainted with such Churches, have little or no idea what is their genesis, and what the special message they have for the religious world of our day.   I have sought to make plain and intelligible for such, a system of belief and practice which has now been preached for just over a century and a half, and which at the present time binds together nearly two million Christians in a single fellowship.

But there is a second reason which has called for the writing of this book. Most Protestant Churches to-day are suffering from a lack of what may be called " church consciousness," and this is felt amongst Churches of Christ. Such a lack is indeed likely to occur at that stage in the history of a movement at which we find ourselves. During the first and second generations in any movement, especially in religious movements, there is usually a clear understanding, amongst the majority of the members, of the great principles and special tenets for which the movement stands. But during the course of its history such a movement attracts to itself men and women, who, having been trained in other schools, lack this clear perception. They bring with them much from their old associations, and are seldom aware that some things to which they tenaciously cling, may in many cases have no relevance to, and in other cases be directly opposed to, the new faith which they have adopted. Especially is this danger present in a movement which, like the one we are describing, has persistently refused to formulate its beliefs and practices in a written creed or confession. Hence development takes place within the movement. This development, in itself, as in the early days of Christianity, may be a good thing. But there also arises a general haziness of belief and sometimes an almost total lack of understanding as to what is to be accepted as of the Faith. That this haziness is being felt in the Churches to-day is generally admitted. And so an attempt has been made to meet the needs of young Church members and others, that they may be able to give a " reason for the hope that is in them." It is possible, in this connection, that the book may help to bring about a revival of those days when every Christian was an *instructed* Christian, and a missionary for the Faith.

Further, it will be obvious that the book has been written for two classes of readers. In the main I have had in mind those without any technical training in theology, philosophy, or Church history, and I hope that none such will find any difficulty in the pages which follow. But I have also had in mind those who possess such technical training, and I have added certain matter and referred to certain works (mostly in footnotes) for their benefit. The reader without technical training would best *read the book through without paying any attention to the foot-notes*. In this way he will avoid meeting difficulties, and so grasp the essential message which I have tried to convey.

The book has been written at the request of the Publishing Committee of the Churches of Christ in Great Britain and Ireland, and its contents revised, first by a small sub-committee and then by the full committee. It is not therefore a personal statement. I have thought it best to treat the subject historically, but I have also kept steadily before me the aim of expressing in modern terms those fundamental beliefs and practices, which the exponents of the Churches' faith, past and present, would agree was the essential message of the Churches of Christ. A quality *par excellence* which every historian must possess is that of *sympathy*, and I trust that, having been nurtured in the Faith, and having spent seventy years within the fold of the Church—forty of these in active service—I may claim some measure of this sympathy and understanding. At least I can claim that quality which all true sympathy must possess—the quality of love for the Movement, to whose message I am seeking to give a wider publicity. Without this quality no man should essay the task of description or criticism ; with it he may hope to be successful in both. Moreover I am fully conscious of the great honour the Publishing Committee have conferred upon me, in asking me to be their mouthpiece on this occasion. The task has not been an easy one, but it has been a labour of love and has brought me much joy. Before closing this Foreword, there are two things I ought to say to those who stand outside the Movement. The first is to explain in what sense the term " Churches of Christ " is used. I know that to many the use of the name savours of arrogance ; but I wish to assure all, that it is never used by us in any arrogant way. The expression is merely used out of a sincere desire to avoid denominational names and party spirit amongst those who should be " one in Christ Jesus our Lord." It has been usual for us to say that we do not claim to be "*the only* Churches of Christ," but " Churches of Christ *only*," and I do not know how it could be better said.[1]   What better

[1] See *The Faith and Practice of Certain Churches of Christ*, by Lancelot Oliver, p. 5.

8

name could be given to that Divine Society, of which Jesus Christ is Head, than " Church of Christ ? " May we not hope that the day is fast coming when all bodies of Christians will take an initial step towards unity by dropping local and party names ? We have recently seen signs of this in Canada, and South India. Certainly those who call themselves Churches of Christ in this country would rejoice if this step were taken.

Secondly, " it should be remembered, especially by those who read this book and hear of the Churches of Christ for the first time, that it is one thing to have ' a knowledge of the truth,' and another thing to practise it. It may be possible, therefore, for a visitor to a Church of Christ, as in the case of any other Christian body, to be disappointed at the standard of Christianity attained by that Church or by individual members of it ; and in consequence to throw aside the truths contained in these pages, as of no account. That would be as wise a procedure as to burn the New Testament, because a man, coming from a professedly Christian country, is seen by a native of another country living in notorious sin. The New Testament cannot be responsible for the unworthiness of those who professedly accept its teaching. Neither can the truths urged by Churches of Christ be set aside because individual members, or a Church here and there, do not come up to the highest standard. What is urged is that the truth set forth in this book does represent an honest and straightforward attempt to understand and interpret the Scriptures ; an attempt which has given rise to the founding of Churches of Christ in many parts of the world, and it is submitted that it is worthy of careful thought and consideration."[1]

Finally I wish to acknowledge my indebtedness to several who have helped me ; to the Sub-Committee—the late Mr. Joseph Smith, Lecturer in Old Testament and Hebrew in Overdale College, the late Mr. Albert Brown, Editor of the *Christian Advocate*, and the late Mr. Edmund Hicken, all of whom have given me valuable advice and criticism;[2] to many members of the Publishing Committee ; and to Mr. Jas. Gray, M.A.,[3] one of my own students, for considerable assistance in proof-reading.

W.R.

OVERDALE COLLEGE,
   Easter 1926.

[1] I am indebted for these words to the late Mr. E. H. Spring, of the Church at Gloucester. They are eminently sane and should be borne in mind by all readers.

[2] All of whom have since died (1947).

[3] Late Warden of Overdale College.

WHAT CHURCHES OF CHRIST STAND FOR

Chapter I

THE BEGINNINGS OF A NEW MOVEMENT IN TWO CONTINENTS

To the average man of this practical western world of ours, the thinker—or as he is sometimes called, the philosopher—has very little, if anything, to do with the changes, whether political or religious, which have been, or are being wrought out in actual life. But it is certain that the average man is wrong. It is a moot question whether history gives rise to philosophy or philosophy to history, but it is certain that the two are very closely connected, whether we think of religious or of secular history. The thinker, or philosopher, may seem to be a man very much up in the clouds, and it may take some time for his philosophy to wield its influence on the concrete things of every day life. He may even need a " populariser " or several generations of " popularisers." But in the end, although it may be difficult for some of us to see it, he is the chief instrument in raising up institutions and changing the course of events, either for good or for evil.

History itself is best described as a series of movements. In every realm of life there are periods of ease and stagnation, and periods of change and growth when activity is everywhere present. Such periods of growth usually mean confusion in the realm of thought and chaos in the realm of practical life. They usually, however, make for advance, but this is not inevitable.[1] The close of the eighteenth and the beginning of the nineteenth century was such a period. In the realm of philosophy, Rationalism and Empiricism had run their course, and had produced in the religious world a condition of stagnation, which is well described by Butler in his *Analogy*, and perhaps better in his Sermons. Deism in this country—both in the Established Church and among the Dissenters—had resulted in *religion* being displaced by a purely reasoned *theology*, based on what can best be described as the ideas of an absentee God, and a self-sufficient humanity. Logic was supreme. But logic had to give place to reality ; and the system was altogether out of touch with the deeper emotions and needs of man, which though they may slumber for a season, at length demand attention and cry out for satisfaction.

Long before the close of the eighteenth century Rationalism and Empiricism were out of

[1] See what I have said in *Religion and Life*, pp. 13 ff.

tune with the world of human needs, though they were to provide the foundation for the work of the Industrial Revolution, and the progress in science which characterised the Victorian age. Hence the rise of Romanticism, which has had such potent results, not only in the sphere of religion, but in the spheres of art and literature. The Methodist Revival, in this country and in America, Pietism and the work of Schleiermacher on the Continent, the rise of the Evangelicals in the Established Church of England, and later the Catholic Revival under Newman, Pusey, and Keble, were all expressions in the religious sphere of the movement we call Romanticism in the realm of philosophy. So were the writings of Scott, Wordsworth, Shelley, Keats, and a dozen others, in the realm of literature.[1]

Wesley, who caught some of his zeal and enthusiasm from the Moravians, who in turn owed much to the German Pietists, was reacting against the cold dry intellectualism, and self-satisfied worldliness of the great bulk of the Anglican Church. It was a healthy reaction,

---

[1] Of course the great blow to Rationalism was struck by Immanuel Kant, who laid the seeds of almost every modern philosophy. Schleiermacher, and later Ritschl, both of whom in different senses may be said to be the fathers of liberal theology, owed much to him. To put it simply, Kant had stressed both the will and the emotions as against the intellect. Schleiermacher, in the realm of religion, placed all his emphasis on the emotions ; Ritschl mainly on the will. Both strove to free religion and theology from the domination of metaphysics. Both Mediæval Scholasticism, and the later Protestant Scholasticism, which were dominated by Rationalism, had made religion subservient to metaphysics.

and he not only succeeded remarkably in his own work, but he gave new life and energy to the Nonconformists of his day. This was the age which saw the birth of Protestant missions, and the rise of many movements for the redress of social evils. Sunday Schools ushered in a new age of education, and the first blows were struck at the gigantic slavery evil. Men began to see visions and to dream dreams.

But it was also an age of *confusion*, and nowhere was this confusion so apparent as in the religious world, and perhaps in no country so much as in the American States. Enthusiasm ran wild. Emotionalism triumphed over the intellect. At the beginning of the nineteenth century, religious men in many parts of America had lost their sanity. There was, in most places, a total lack of organised religious effort. Sects were everywhere. Bitterness and hatred between them was the rule. New prophets, each with some fantastic interpretation of the Bible, were constantly arising, and in most cases, even the prophets themselves had no real knowledge of the Bible. Their systems were usually founded on the interpretation of one or two obscure texts, chosen indiscriminately from any part of the sacred Book. Impromptu camp meetings with wild emotionalism and often gross im- morality, which usually accompanies such scenes, were the rule of the day. There were Seventh Day Baptists, Free Will Baptists, Hard Shell Baptists, Soft Shell Baptists, Glory Alleluia

Baptists, Perfectionists, Shakers, Comers Out, and a hundred other varieties of pseudo-Christianity, all of which claimed an infallibility peculiar to themselves. Such was the harvest which was reaped from the wave of emotionalism which swept over Europe and America. It was a harvest due very largely to the fact that things were in the hands of ignorant and self-appointed men, with minds totally unaccustomed to grapple with theological difficulties. Most of them had but the slightest acquaintance with the elements of the Christian Faith itself, but possessed a good deal of natural ability and sheer force of personality.[1]

Among the more organised bodies themselves, there was a great deal of bitterness and party strife. The method of toleration had given place to religious bigotry and sectarian zeal of a very unlovely type. One good thing may be said about it all. Indifference had gone. There was a zeal for something, even if that something were wrong. Undoubtedly there was much charlatanism, but the condition of affairs itself witnessed to a real interest in vital things, and was the expression of a deep-felt need of humanity, only dimly conscious of its own nature, seeking to express itself in manifold forms.

It was on the background of all this bitter sectarian strife, with its many new systems of

[1] See *Religion Follows The Frontier*, by W. E. Garrison, and *Adventuring for Christian Unity*, by Dean E. Walker.

Christianity, most of them weird and curious, that there arose the Movement we are to consider. It is not to be classed amongst the peculiar bodies and sects we have enumerated, nor amongst others of a similar type which arose later. Rather it came into being as a reaction against them, and *against all narrow bigotry* in the sphere of religion. It was in its essence a movement for catholicism in the sense of universalism, against all forms of sectarianism. It was also a movement for a sane and reasoned *New Testament theology*, against the terrible outcrop of *isms* which a too one-sided emotionalism had produced. And moreover, both in America and in England, where it arose simultaneously in the early years of the nineteenth century, it was guided and directed by *trained minds*—theologically trained so far as this country is concerned, and both theologically and philosophically trained so far as America is concerned. This historic background should never be forgotten, for it forms the key to the interpretation of all that follows.

In America the Movement had a double origin, and each was independent of the other. In 1801 Barton W. Stone, a Presbyterian minister of Cane Ridge, Kentucky, caused grave trouble by uniting with Baptist and Methodist preachers in a great revival, of which he writes, " The roads were literally crowded with wagons, carriages, horsemen and footmen, moving to the solemn camp. The sight was affecting . . . . .

there were between twenty and thirty thousand collected." As a result, one of his colleagues, Richard McNemar, also a Presbyterian minister, was cited before the Lexington Presbytery for affiliating with ministers of another communion. This led to the formation of the Springfield Presbytery by McNemar, Stone and others, a Presbytery which sought to protest against all religious bigotry. But Stone and his colleagues, having taken this step, were led on to make a further study of New Testament teaching concerning the Church of Christ, and this led, in 1804 to the dissolution of the Springfield Presbytery, and a call was made to men and women to take the name of Christian only and the " Bible as the only sure guide to heaven, without any mixture of philosophy, vain deceit, traditions of men or rudiments of the world."[1] So arose, through force of circumstances, a number of Churches, mostly in the State of Kentucky, wearing the name of Christ only, of which Stone was the revered leader. It was not until 1835 that this branch of the Movement came into union with another of which we shall now speak. A close union was effected which has never since been dissolved.

Thomas Campbell was born in County Down, Ireland, in 1763, and educated at Glasgow University for the Presbyterian ministry. In early life he seems to have been deeply grieved by the divisions in Christendom, and by terrible

---

[1] See the strange document, *The Last Will and Testament of the Springfield Presbytery*.

exhibitions of bigotry often amounting to fanaticism. In 1807 he emigrated to America, and settled as a Presbyterian minister in Washington County, Pennsylvania. Here he began to work for Christian Union and the *breaking down of party bigotry*, and as a result came under suspicion of the Presbytery. He went so far as to fellowship with Christians of other denominations. For this he was censured by the Chartiers Presbytery, but an appeal to the North American Synod brought about his acquittal, but opposition against him became more and more bitter, forcing him at last to withdraw from the Presbyterian Church. Already he had enunciated the principles, " Where the Scriptures speak we speak, and where they are silent we are silent," and " Christian liberality and Christian Union on the basis of the Bible," little dreaming where these principles would lead him. The decisive date in the history of this movement has usually been taken to be 1809 when Campbell issued " A Declaration and Address," and formed the Christian Association of Washington. It was not in any sense a Church, but rather a Society on the model of the early Methodist societies.[1] The Declaration renounced all systems of theology *as tests of fellowship*, and, as we shall see, this has *remained a characteristic feature* of the teaching of Churches of Christ.

In this year, 1809, Thomas Campbell was

[1] See *A Declaration and Address*, by Thomas Campbell.

joined by his son Alexander, who was destined to become the chief leader in the Movement.[1] Alexander had studied at Glasgow University, and had there come into contact with the work of the Haldanes. He was a thoroughly well-equipped scholar in the classics, theology, and philosophy ; and already, whilst in Scotland, had come to hold views about sectarianism and the evils of division similar to those held by his father. So that when he joined his father, the latter was happy to find his son in such complete agreement with his ideals. Alexander threw himself whole-heartedly into the work. Campbell still shrank from forming a separate community and now sought admission to the more liberal synod of Pittsburg, but he was refused, mainly it would seem for " opposing creeds and confessions as injurious to the interests of religion." So in 1810, very reluctantly, he organised his community at Brush Run into a Church. It was not, however, until June 12, 1812, that Campbell and his son were convinced of the unscriptural character of Infant Baptism, and were baptised (immersed) on a public confession of the Lordship of Jesus. But the Campbells were very loth to start a new organisa-tion, and in 1813 they associated themselves with the Redstone Baptist Association. It should, however, be clearly understood that the

[1] See *Encyclopædia Britannica*, and *Harmsworth Encyclopædia :* articles *Alexander Campbell. The World's Great Sermons* includes a sermon by Alexander Campbell.

Movement we are considering, so far as America is concerned, did not take its rise from the Baptist, but from the Presbyterian Church. The home of the Campbells within the Baptist fold was quite temporary, and their sojourn was far from happy. They had little affinity with the Baptists of that day, except the practice of Believers' Baptism.[1] These American Baptists looked with suspicion upon all learned men, whereas the Campbells were both *highly educated*. A rift was caused when, in 1816, A. Campbell delivered his *Sermon on the Law*,[2] which emphasised the Pauline teaching that Christians are entirely free from the Law of Moses. In those days such teaching was considered most heretical. But his influence gradually widened throughout the Southern States. In 1820 he was joined by Walter Scott,[3] who had been educated for the Presbyterian ministry in the University of Edinburgh, and in 1823 both sought refuge in the more liberal Mahoning Baptist Association. But the Redstone Association still pursued its exclusive policy and in 1826 excommunicated fourteen Churches. In 1823 Campbell started the *Christian Baptist*, a monthly

[1] See Prof. Curtis, *History of Creeds and Confessions of Faith*, p. 307, who inadvertently makes a mistake here. He even links Churches of Christ with Plymouth Brethren, a body of people with whom they have *no sort of connection*, either doctrinally or historically.

[2] Which see.

[3] See *The Messiahship*. He is perhaps as much the founder of the new Movement as the Campbells. It is almost certain that he was responsible for A. Campbell adopting the more Catholic doctrine of Baptism—that it is " for the remission of sins."

publication, which ran into seven volumes.[1] This was followed in 1830 by the *Millennial Harbinger*.[2] In 1832 the temporary association of the Campbells and Scott with the Baptists ended, and *against their own will* these leaders were forced to organise a separate community. That year Campbell wrote " All the world must see that we have been forced into a separate communion." Thus arose the separate body known in America as " Disciples of Christ." In 1835 Campbell produced his *Christian System*, a learned work running into some 350 pages.[3]

In the British Isles the origin of the Movement was somewhat different. The beginnings go back much further, and many streams unite to form what has been an organised body, at least from 1842, when the first Annual Conference of Churches was held in Edinburgh. The beginnings are more difficult to trace ; they are not so

[1] These are published in one volume, and in them his constructive theology is worked out.

[2] It should be pointed out that this title has no reference to what we now call Millenarian views.

[3] The *Christian System* is the classic of what has often been called the " Restoration Movement." Its style is of course that of its own day, and its terms are not those which are in common use with us, whilst its philosophical background reflects, in the main, the teaching of Locke and the English school of Empirical-Rationalists. These facts combined, tend to make the book somewhat difficult for a modern reader, but once this initial difficulty has been mastered, it will present few obstacles to a thoughtful reader. The book is the work of a master mind. At more than one point Mr. Campbell shows himself to have been before his time. This is particularly so in his interpretation of Holy Scripture. He anticipates one of the fundamental principles of the Tübingen School by ten years. It is to be regretted that this work is so little read and studied by Church members in these days. The result is a great deal of loose talk, and loose thinking which is regrettable.

localised as in America, and growth has been by no means so rapid. There are some Churches still in existence whose history goes back well into the last half of the eighteenth century, I speak now of British Churches.

In one sense the Churches in this country owe their origin to the Glasites or Sandemanians.[1] John Glas (1695-1773) was a Presbyterian minister of the Established Church of Scotland, who was deposed in 1730 for opposing state alliance. Robert Sandeman (1723-1771) was his son-in-law, and both pleaded for a "return to the simple beliefs and ways of New Testament Christians." They established a weekly celebration of the Lord's Supper, and stressed the *intellect* as against the *emotions*; both of which things were characteristic of Campbell's teaching.[2] They practised many other excellent things, and set up a form of Church government consisting of Presbyters and Deacons in each Church with liberty of teaching for qualified male members outside the official ministry. Quite a number of distinguished people were Glasites, amongst them Michael Faraday the scientist.

Archibald McLean (1733-1812) was a learned Glasite who came to renounce pædo-Baptist views, and was baptised in 1765 by Robert

[1] See *Transactions of the Baptist Historical Society*, Vol. VII.; article by the late Prof. T. Witton Davies, D.D. See also *Encyclopædia of Religion and Ethics*; article *Glasites*.

[2] It is of course clear to us, looking back, that their attack on the emotional element in religious experience was one-sided.

Carmichael, another former Glasite minister.[1] These two formed a Scotch Baptist Church in Edinburgh that year. McLean influenced William Jones, M.A., who later became minister of a Scotch Baptist Church in London.[2] Both McLean and William Jones had great influence on the Baptist Churches in Wales, especially on J. R. Jones (1765-1834) of Ramoth, one of the greatest of Welsh preachers. He again was friendly with Dr. William Richards of Lynn, Norfolk, who by 1818 had imbibed McLeanist views. It is also certain that not later than 1801 there were definite Scotch (McLeanist) Baptist Churches in Wales, and it was these Churches, amongst Welsh Baptists, which later were influenced by the teachings of Campbell.

In the main, then, it may be said that Churches of Christ in this country came into existence as a result of the work of Scotch (McLeanist) Baptists ; though a number of other isolated Churches in England, Scotland, and Ireland had, independently, from the late years of the eighteenth century onwards, reached the same position. The most outstanding figure other than that of Wm. Jones is James Wallis,[3] of

---

[1] See the *Works of A. McLean* (7 vols.).

[2] Jones came into contact with A. Campbell's writings in the early thirties, and made them familiar to English readers in the *Millennial Harbinger* (2 vols., 1835-36). He died in 1846, the year before Campbell visited this country. See also his *Primitive Christianity*, 1837.

[3] See the *Christian Messenger* (12 vols., 1837-45), which Wallis along with others issued in order to carry on the work of making A. Campbell's views known—a work which owing to ill-health Wm. Jones, M.A., had had to relinquish. This was followed by the *British Millennial Harbinger*, which Wallis at first edited.

Nottingham, who in 1836 formed a Church which in the main stood for the same things for which Campbell was then contending in America. In 1842 the Edinburgh Conference showed a list of fifty Churches taking the name " Church of Christ " only, pleading for the abolition of sectarianism, and a unified Church, by a return to the faith and practice of Apostolic Christianity. The next Conference was held in Chester in 1847, when A. Campbell himself was Chairman, and eighty Churches were on the list.

So began a remarkable religious movement in two continents—a movement with *a passion for the unity of the Body of Christ, an abhorrence of sectarianism and all party spirit, and a deep conviction that no unity could be achieved until the life, faith, and order of the New Testament Church were restored.*[1]

[1] See the *Encyclopædia of Religion and Ethics ;* article *Disciples of Christ.* See also *A History of the Christian Church*, by Williston Walker, p. 581.

CHAPTER II

GROWTH AND DEVELOPMENT

WHAT then has been the outcome of the Movement whose beginnings we have outlined? Like all other movements, it has had its periods of stagnation, and there have been times of difficulty marked by controversy, but throughout a century's history there have never been wanting those signs of growth and development which characterise all living bodies, as contrasted with those which are dead or dying. In a very real sense there has been *movement*. We have only room for the briefest statement of development.

So far as the British Isles is concerned, we have seen that the Movement began with a *stressing of intellectual values*. Its beginnings were scholarly in the best sense of the word, and this is witnessed to by all the early literature, by the writings of McLean, Jones, and Wallis. In the main it seems to have attracted real *Bible students* and *thinkers*. It was not in any sense " popular," and never attempted to make any " popular " appeal. Men and women joined the Churches out of conviction, and very often this meant a real sacrifice in more than one way. There was a quiet, restrained dignity about it all, marked by sanity and an absence of sentimentalism.

But from the beginning it was anti-clerical, in the sense of reacting against professionalism in the ministry, and it naturally attracted to its fold many who had this same sympathy, but who lacked the rational temper, which had disciplined the early founders of the Churches.[1] This eventually led to a loss of touch with modern scholarship, both secular and theological, and an indifference as to forms of ministry in the Church.[2] All this was influenced by two other factors. The first was the experience of the Churches in America, where a large number of colleges had been formed, with the result that in a number of Churches preaching had practically become confined to the trained ministry—a position which the Churches in this country sought to avoid at all costs. The second was what Mr. David King, who, more than any other man, during the last half of the nineteenth

[1] This reaction never completely captured the Churches, as is seen by the fact that training work has always been carried on, first under Mr. David King, and Mr. Alexander Brown ; and later under Mr. Lancelot Oliver, and Mr. John M'Cartney.

[2] This indifference to forms of ministry is witnessed to by Mr. James Anderson in his *Outline of my Life*, p. 184. In some Churches the position almost approximated to that of the Quakers, though never quite, and there was a widespread rejection of ordination. So strong was the reaction against a *professional* ministry, that members of Churches were fairly numerous who would have said that Churches of Christ had no ministry ; whereas the original position was that of Bishops and Deacons ordained in each local Church.

century moulded the thought of the Churches, called the " Plymouthian leaven."[1] The claim was more and more stressed, as it had been by many of the Reformers in the sixteenth century, that every man was capable of interpreting the New Testament for himself, and so reconstructing the Christian System. Colleges were generally looked upon with suspicion, and amongst some such things as the use of instrumental music in worship, Sunday Schools, and Foreign Missions were regarded as doubtful expedients. The original Movement had been a *challenge to think* but, as in all movements, the period of crystallisation set in, and to some extent a set of beliefs and practices became the accepted rule, from which there must be no departure, although the old antipathy to a written creed was never broken down. There was, however, a tendency—though it was by no means general—to be satisfied with the truth as it had been discovered, and to regard it as final. This again led to lack of emphasis on Christian Unity (the very passion of the original Movement), which was accompanied by a loss of vision and of catholicity of spirit. The attitude was not so much that of a seeker after truth as that of a possessor of truth

---

[1] See *Memoirs of David King*, pp. 239 ff. Mr. King was in many ways a most remarkable man, keenly intellectual and a born leader. He debated successfully with Bradlaugh. He lamented the " Plymouthian leaven," and assigned it to the publication of *The Messiah's Ministry*, by T. H. Milner, who had at one time been amongst the Brethren. Mr. King claimed that had Mr. Milner lived longer, he would have revised his book very seriously.

that must be handed on.[1]   It was inevitable that this should be so ; for it would seem that there are times when truth can only be preserved in this way, and moreover it should be remembered that the spirit of the age manifested in the Christian world of this period was that of denominational rivalry.

In passing we may note also some measure of failure to give attention to modes of worship and to the corporate satisfaction of spiritual instincts. The methods of the lecture hall, where the message had been preached in the early days, were carried over to some extent when permanent chapels came to be built.

Some fifty years ago two new forces were at work within the Movement. Largely owing to the work of Mr. Sydney Black, there started a revival along evangelical lines—a quickening of the pulse.[2]   The revival was marked by great zeal and enthusiasm.   This new force and new direction in thought and effort had a very wide-

---

[1] But that this was by no means the attitude of leaders in the Movement is shown by the following words of Mr. Lancelot Oliver, Editor of the *Bible Advocate :* " We have never held that a return to New Testament Christianity and acceptance of what we think constitutes it, are necessarily one and the same thing ; and at needed moments the fact has been recalled that we must ever be ready to diminish or enlarge, as further truth breaks forth from God's Word. Indeed nothing is absolutely and ultimately binding but *truth,* so that Christianity itself must be abandoned were it proved to be false.   But when it is held that certain things are true, and a serious attempt made to consider objections as they arise, it is surely our duty to press what we hold as truth, all we can, undeterred by a possible future discovery that we are in error " (May 6, 1910).   See also *New Testament Christianity*, p. 203.

[2] See *Life of Sydney Black*, by T. J. Ainsworth.

spread effect for good, but it also had its own peculiar dangers.[1] It was set against the narrow literalism of which we have spoken, but in some places, where its influence was widely felt, there was a danger that the original fundamental message for which the Churches had stood should be lost in a common form of Evangelicalism. Undoubtedly a number, who knew little of the special witness to which they were heirs, were added to the Churches. To some extent there resulted a lack of emphasis on Church order, and to a less extent on the sacraments. What had been termed *definite* teaching was not now so much in favour. There resulted a lack of Church consciousness, and a tendency to vagueness ; and yet, the main result was good ; for it produced a far more catholic spirit and a readiness to join with other Christians in the great work of fighting social evils. And throughout it all, the Churches never lost their essential witness to the necessity for New Testament Christianity, to the unity of Christ's Body the Church, to the restoration of the sacraments to their rightful place, and to the necessity of using the gifts of every member in the service of the Church.

Side by side with this revival, came one demanding a more liberal attitude to scholarship. A new magazine was started called *The Young Christian*, but it had only a short life. The

---

[1] Of these dangers, those who were responsible for this awakening in the Churches were fully aware, and sought in every way to guard against them.

effort met with little favour; for by this time the Churches had largely forgotten their own origin and the scholarly beginnings from which they had sprung, but it paved the way for what was to follow. And so we pass rapidly on to the present time, when the full fruit of these two stirrings within the Churches is being reaped. The last forty years has not been a period of growth in numbers, but it has seen many new developments. Chief amongst these has been the establishing of a Theological College in Birmingham, where men receive a four years' (sometimes longer, sometimes shorter) course of training. Here the findings of modern scholarship have been brought to bear on the Church's special witness, with the result that all that is of value within it has been strengthened and enriched. This we shall see in the chapters which follow. New efforts in publishing are on foot. A Summer School in Theology is held annually, as well as a Men's Convention and a Women's Convention for the study of social and theological questions. Youth Work is also organised under a Fellowship of Youth which has an Annual Convention. It means that the Movement is once again giving to scholarship its proper place, and is finding itself, and re-interpreting its essential message in the new religious world into which we have all been ushered during the past three-quarters of a century.

During this time, too, there have been other activities which have witnessed to life within the Movement. Sunday Schools had existed from earliest times, and definite organised work was begun as long ago as 1872. From that time a General Committee has given attention to this work alone. Largely owing to the enthusiasm of the late Mr. James Flisher, of Manchester, who late in life was trained at Westhill, the work of organisation, especially that of grading, has gone forward rapidly, and there has been little opposition.

For quite a long time Missions Overseas were not begun, but in 1892 organised work was started, and now a vigorous Committee carries on operations in three fields, Siam, India, and Central Africa. Social work, too, especially Temperance and Peace propaganda, is well organised and supported by the Churches.

So far as America is concerned development and growth have been far more rapid. From the first, stress was placed on education, and so a large number of colleges arose supported by the Churches. There have, however, been movements away from this policy especially in the Southern States, but they are not relatively important. Growth has been very rapid, so that to-day " Disciples " (as they are usually called) hold the fifth position amongst Protestant communities in the States. As in most religious bodies there, three parties can be clearly defined : (a) the ultra-conservative party, (b) a middle party who accept in the main the results of modern scholarship, and retain and stress in a catholic spirit the essential witness of the Disciples, (c) the left wing of liberals, who are mainly represented in and around Chicago. But all these tendencies do not lead to any separation in the organised body. The American Churches have large Mission Stations in many parts of Asia, and in Africa and South America.

The Movement has spread to the Dominions, Australia, New Zealand, and South Africa, largely owing to the efforts of the British Churches. In later years Australia and Africa have come under the influence of the American Churches. In Canada there has been both American and British effort at work.

Here, the growth numerically has not been rapid. To-day there are over 9,000 members with 123 Churches. A Theological College has been in existence for twenty-five years, and there is a vigorous publishing department. In America there are about one and a half million members with over thirty Colleges and Universities. Australia has over 30,000 with a well-established Theological College in Melbourne, and at present very rapid growth is taking place. New Zealand has nearly 5,000 members, with a Theological College in Dunedin. Altogether, after a century's work, there are some two million Christians pleading for the unity of the Church by a return to New Testament Christianity.

And what can we say of the men produced by this Movement ? It is only possible to mention a few of those whose names have not so far come before us. Of statesmen the most noteworthy is President Garfield, loved throughout the American States. In this country Lloyd George was reared in the little Church at Criccieth, of which his uncle (a most remarkable personality) was co-Elder throughout a very long life.

Amongst scholars there have been many in America; and in this country a number will remember with gratitude Mr. J. B. Rotherham, the translator of the Emphasised Bible, and Professor Joseph Smith, author of *Synoptic Tables*. The Movement has not been without its mystics and poets, men of deep religious piety. And here we must mention Mr. G. Y. Tickle, Mr. Joseph Adam, and Mr. Joseph Collin, men who have enriched hymnody by their productions.

We have sought to outline briefly the rise and development of a significant religious Movement, whose growth has been phenomenal. In the following chapters we shall try to make clear what is the essential message of this Movement for the world of to-day.

CHAPTER III

THE SIGNIFICANCE OF THE NEW TESTAMENT

IN this and the following seven chapters (III-X) we shall outline the contributions which Churches of Christ have made to the religious thinking of their day. Happily, as we shall show, in some cases, the matters with which the chapters deal no longer constitute marks of distinction between these Churches and other religious bodies ; but for a complete understanding of this Movement we must realise, nevertheless, that these chapters, in the main, cover its distinctive features.

We must begin with the *position of the New Testament ;* for this is the key to the whole situation. Whether we think of England or America the key-note was a *restoration of New Testament Christianity*. To grasp the significance of this, we must think ourselves back into the early years of the nineteenth century. The Reformers of the sixteenth century had had the same motive, and they achieved some measure of success. It was, however, a partial success ; for in each case their systems had been crystallised and summed up in creeds and confessions, most of them abstruse, lengthy, and conditioned by the theological disputations of their day. We in the twentieth century have lived to see the day when such creeds and confessions are, in the main, looked upon as a burden. But a century ago they were as tenaciously held as the Mediæval Catholic system had been held against the Reformers.[1] On the other hand there had begun, as we have noticed, a reaction against this credalised form of Protestantism—a wild untutored reaction, which based itself on experience, and which had resulted in a large number of *isms* and strange beliefs.

Against this the Campbells urged that the unity of the Church could only be secured by abandoning the confessions and formularies on the one hand, and the theories of infallible guidance by the Holy Spirit on the other. They pleaded for a return to the faith and practice of the Church as founded and perfected by the Apostles of our Lord. Note also that it was *New* Testament Christianity for which they pleaded. It should be remembered that at this time, and for many years later, any belief or practice was supported by an indiscriminate reference to Scripture, no matter from what book the text came—Genesis, Ecclesiastes, or Romans were equally valuable. The Bible was little known as an *historical* book. Campbell in his day was doing much the same thing as Stephen in

[1] The Protestantism of Campbell's day was as scholastic as Mediæval Catholicism. It was not based on experience as it largely is to-day.

35

Jerusalem, or Paul in the Galatian and Roman Epistles. When he preached his "Sermon on the Law." he was expelled from the Baptist Association in which he had temporarily found a refuge. In this sermon he distinguished sharply between the Old and New Covenants, and clearly demonstrated that we as Christians are not under the Law of Moses. He claimed that the scholastic distinction between the *ceremonial* and *moral* law, which Protestants had widely adopted (maintaining that the old *moral* law was binding, though the *ceremonial* law was not), was a false distinction and alien to the thought and spirit of the New Testament, and especially of Paul.[1] But this was heresy in the Protestant world of his day ! To-day we can rejoice that for most instructed Christians it is common ground.

But the early reformers of the nineteenth century went further than this. They were opposed to the method of *textual theology* then so prevalent ; that is, they opposed the quoting of texts apart from their contexts and historic settings. The Bible to them was an *historical* book and was to be interpreted as other ancient books were interpreted. Campbell said, " On opening any book in the sacred Scriptures *consider first the historical circumstances of the book. These are the order, the title, the author, the date, the place, and the occasion of it ;* " and again, " The date, place, and occasion of it, are obviously

---

[1] A position which has since been upheld by modern O.T. scholarship.

necessary to a right application of anything in the book."[1]   Here was sanity indeed. What a mass of mistakes the religious world would have been saved from if this principle had been followed !

Campbell recognised, too, a sphere for *development*, for he, and all the reformers, drew a sharp distinction in matters of Church order and discipline between the realms of order and expediency, between what was merely temporary and what permanent, between faith and opinion. Nothing was to be considered as of the Faith except that which had the clear warrant of New Testament teaching.   They pleaded, too, for the giving up of abstruse theological terms, and for the adopting of New Testament language in speaking of the great doctrines and ordinances of the Church ; a plea which is now being urged by theologians of all schools.

It is sometimes said that Protestantism substituted an infallible Book for an infallible Church. This is not altogether true, although there is a measure of truth in it. But the early reformers of the nineteenth century were under no delusions on this matter. They realised that the Scriptures of the New Testament arose in the bosom of the Church, and gave the same honour to the Divine Society as to the Divine Word.[2] Campbell categorically stated, " It is not the will

[1] *Christian System*, p. 16 (1835 Edition).
[2] See my article on " Disciples " in *Ministry and Sacraments*, edited by the Bishop of Gloucester and Dr. Dunkerley.

of Jesus Christ, because it is not adapted to human nature, nor to the present state of His kingdom as administered in His absence, that the Church should be governed by a *written* document alone."[1] This I take to mean that he recognised a region of expediency, where the Church was free to legislate for its own needs. Whilst he rightly exalted the New Testament to the supreme place as witnessing to the nature of Apostolic Christianity, yet at the same time he insisted on its being interpreted *historically ;* that is, he strongly objected to taking texts out of their setting and quoting them indiscriminately, without any reference to the book from which they were taken, or the historical circumstances lying behind the writing of the book. He was also a keen textual critic and edited a new version of the New Testament, and he presumed to subject to critical investigation the historical evidence for the Canon of Holy Scripture.

On all these points the early reformers were misunderstood by their contemporaries, and unjustly accused of heresies of which they were in no sense guilty. Their clear distinction between the Old and New Testaments led to the charge that they rejected the former—an utterly false charge, and a misunderstanding into which the more enlightened world of to-day would never have fallen. The refusal to be bound by the law of Moses led to the charge which was

---

[1] *Christian System*, p. 173. See further, Chapter VIII of this book.

levelled against Paul himself—that the " Camp-
bellites " (as their enemies called them) were
free to commit immorality. No charge could
have been more false than this, for if there has
been one thing characteristic of the whole
Movement (if I may be allowed to say it) it has
been the high moral standard demanded of its
members. Campbell himself was a great moralist.

Their plea for renouncing the metaphysical
subtleties of the confessions and speaking of the
great verities of the Faith in New Testament
terms[1]—sound and sensible as it is when
followed in the spirit in which it was first
enunciated and not debased by a slavish literalism
—led to their being accused of unsoundness of
views on questions such as the Godhead, the
Deity of Christ, and the Atonement. Against
these utterly false charges, Campbell and Scott
were constantly writing.[2]

The strong emphasis on the Holy Spirit
operating through the Word and through the
Church—which as we have seen was occasioned
by opposition to the weird manifestations which
everywhere were being claimed as due to the
Spirit's influence—was really a plea for sanity ;
but by their enemies it was taken as a denial
that God had anything at all to do with man's
salvation—a denial of grace.[3] This again was
an entire misunderstanding.

[1] To-day theologians of all schools are pleading for this very
thing, and in this we may all rejoice.
[2] See Chapter XI.
[3] See Chapters IV and V.

Lastly, the plea for a restoration of New Testament Christianity was generally understood as a desire to return to the " feeding bottle." As the nineteenth century advanced, with its dogmas of evolution and eternal progress, the religious world in general reflected this attitude, and many scoffed at the very idea of returning to Apostolic Christianity. Such an idea was altogether out of tune with the dominant spirit of the age. According to the current interpretation of the evolutionary idea the highest and the best must be in the future.[1]

But we have lived through this age, and thinking men no longer interpret history in this shallow fashion. The classics of ancient Greece are still classics. Shakespeare is not less than even the greatest of our modern poets. Any Public School boy may know more mathematics than Newton did, but we do not therefore think him a greater mathematician nor regard Newton as obsolete. And in like manner we see clearly, to-day, that the spiritual genius of the New Testament, and of the early Church out of which it sprang, is unique. *If we wish to know*

[1] Dean Inge deals trenchantly with this matter in *Science, Religion, and Reality*, p. 351. He complains of those who are reviving the superstition that in religion the best must always be in the future, and says, " Nobody treats the history of art and poetry in this way, but the delusion has not been completely abandoned in the case of religion. We have discussions on what is supposed to be a serious difficulty in the way of accepting Christianity—that on the Christian hypothesis the highest revelation came to mankind nearly two thousand years ago. The truth is that the great religions—Buddhism, Christianity, and Islam—date from the millennium which ends with the career of Mohammed ; and all of them *were at their best when they were fresh from the mint*."

40

what Christianity is, both in form and spirit, it is to the small yet unparalleled group of documents produced within the bosom of the early Church and within the Apostolic age, inspired by the Spirit of God, and by His providential guidance collected into what we now call the New Testament, and to these documents alone, that we must go, interpreting them in the true spirit of history. And on this point we may rejoice that, to-day, there seems to be no sort of doubt, though we are still met by varying interpretations. Thus far has the principle enunciated by the early reformers of the nineteenth century triumphed, at least in the thinking section of the religious world, though the full fruits will only be realised in succeeding generations.[1]

[1] All schools now, both Catholic and Protestant, unite more and more in emphasising the necessity of finding essential Christianity within the Apostolic Church, and consequently within the written record which that Church produced. It is only necessary to quote a few leading scholars. From the Catholic side we have this from Mr. A. E. J. Rawlinson (the late Bishop of Derby). Speaking of the New Testament he says it is " a standard and norm of all subsequent Christian developments," and that by it " all later developments of Christianity need to be constantly tested and judged" (*Historical Christianity*, p. 17). Everyone knows how earnestly in recent years the late Dr. Gore has pleaded for the same thing, and I cannot do better than quote words from the preface of his recent book, *The Holy Spirit and the Church*. Speaking of Church Unity he is sure that there will be no progress until traditional assumptions are laid aside and men ask, " What is the mind of Christ concerning the propagation of His religion ? " He then goes on to say, " Does it not after all appear to be in a high degree probable that the New Testament documents interpret it aright, and that we cannot get behind them or away from them ? " Perhaps Dr. Barnes, the late Bishop of Birmingham, sums up as well as any one what is being said by Protestant scholars, " Are we in doubt as to some particular aspect of Christian Dogma ? Our final court of appeal is the New Testament. Can we justify some particular kind of worship and allied teaching ? We must find out whether it is consonant with the mind of Christ " (*Modern Churchman*, June, 1922, p. 131). See also Harnack, *What is Christianity* ? Peake, *The Nature of Scripture*.

CHAPTER IV

LAW AND GRACE

WE have already referred to the clear distinction made by the nineteenth century reformers between the Old and New Testament Scriptures, and this involved a further clear distinction (which has always been characteristic of Churches of Christ) between *law* and *grace*, or between the Law and the Gospel. This distinction was most clearly set forth in Alexander Campbell's *Sermon on the Law*, preached before the Redstone Baptist Association on September 1, 1816.[1]

For this sermon Mr. Campbell was impeached for heresy, and when we remember the confusion of thought in the religious world of the day, we can hardly be surprised. There was then little idea of a *progressive* revelation, a conception which the reformers preached in season and out of season. Men were prepared to find all the fully developed Christian dogmas, such as the Trinity and the Incarnation, in remote passages in the book of Genesis ; and, to make the Old

---

[1] Of this sermon, Dr. W. T. Moore says, " It may be regarded as embodying the fundamental ideas of the Reformation for which Mr. Campbell pleaded " (*Lectures on the Pentateuch*, edited by W. T. Moore, p. 266).

Testament square with the New, all kinds of allegorical methods of interpretation were resorted to.[1] Speaking of this kind of tendency Campbell could say, " And what shall we say of the genius who discovered that singing hymns and spiritual songs was prohibited, and the office of the Ruling Elder pointed out in the second commandment ! That dancing and stage plays were prohibited in the seventh : and supporting the Clergy enjoined in the eighth ! "

The Old Testament and the Law of Moses were supposed to contain the Gospel as clearly as the New Testament, if only men would apply the right method of interpretation, *i.e.* the

---

[1] It is clear that in the early days the Church never really solved this problem of the relationship of the Old Testament to its own life. Stephen and Paul fought a battle for freedom, but the full effect of their work was not seen in the earliest days of the Church. Marcion, in the second century, was really fighting the same battle, but his dualism led him into serious error. The Church saved the Old Testament largely by having recourse to the allegorical method of interpretation so favoured by the Alexandrian School. We may be profoundly thankful for this, and yet we cannot but recognise that serious harm to religion and theology was done by the uncritical attitude which the Church adopted. Augustine was sane enough on this point (see his treatise on *The Letter and the Spirit*), but extravagances broke out at the Reformation, when the Old Testament became much more prominent, and the ten commandments were exalted into a position they had not before occupied. Thus a great deal of so-called Christian morality was Old Testament morality, and that of an early type. Livingstone tells how the Dutch colonists of South Africa went about with a Bible under one arm and a rifle under the other, believing that they were God's chosen people sent to exterminate the heathen, and occupy the new Canaan ! The spirit of legalism, and all that Christian apologetic which has been advanced in favour of war and slavery, are largely the fruits of the attitude towards the Old Testament against which Campbell and his followers rebelled. To-day modern scholars have reached the same goal by a somewhat different route.

allegorical. Paul's distinction between the *spirit* and the *letter*,[1] instead of being taken as a distinction between the spheres of *law* and *grace*,[2] was taken as a maxim of scriptural interpretation to be applied rigorously to both Old and New Testaments, so that statements from either Testament, relating some ordinary historical event or ceremonial enactment, did not really mean what they said. They must be *spiritually* interpreted. The result was chaos. Against this the early reformers claimed that the Bible was an *historical* book, and subject to the same laws of interpretation as other historical books. So Campbell said, " We have in the Holy Scriptures, every form of expression. We have not only poetry and prose, precepts, promises, and threats : but all the various forms and usages of human speech ; " and again, " The words and sentences of the Bible are to be translated, interpreted, and understood according to the same code of laws and principles of interpretation by which other ancient writings are translated and understood . . . this is essential to its character as a revelation from God ; otherwise it would be no revelation."[3] They further maintained that the ten commandments were not the *Christian* moral code, and not in any sense binding on Christians. Here are some of

[1] 2 Cor. iii. 6.

[2] See *The Approach to the New Testament*, by Dr. Moffatt, for a sane treatment of " the letter killeth, but the spirit maketh alive."

[3] *Christian System*, pp. 15 f.

44

the things which Campbell said on this point, in the *Sermon on the Law* : " Paul according to the wisdom given unto him, denominated the ten precepts the ' ministration of condemnation and death.' " " Do we not know, with Paul, that what things soever the law saith, it saith to them that are under the law ? But even to the Jews it was not the most suitable rule of life . . . as long as polygamy, divorces, slavery, revenge, etc., were winked at under the law, so long must the lives of its best subjects be stained with glaring imperfections." " The defects of the law are of a relative kind. It is not in itself weak or sinful—some part of it was holy, just, and good —other parts of it were elementary, shadowy representations of good things to come." And so this Movement emphasised once again, to a world which sorely needed it, what Paul had emphasised when he claimed that "with freedom did Christ set us free," and what the writer of Hebrews had claimed—that in Christ the Law was done away. Of course the reformers were met by the usual charges about immorality—the claim that if the law was not binding, then men might conduct themselves pretty much as they chose. To these charges they replied that the legalistic form of morality contained in the Law had no value for Christians—it was primitive— and far inferior to that law of union with Christ, in which a man becomes dead unto sin. And like Augustine they laid stress on the two-fold law of love to God and our fellow-men as a natural

standard of duty underlying all moral obligation.[1]
Several things have resulted from this sane
attitude towards the Old Testament and the Law.

(a) Churches of Christ have never been
Sabbatarian, and their well-instructed
members have never fallen a prey to
either Sabbatarian sentimentalism, or to
the various cults of Seventh Day
Adventism. The Churches have always
clearly distinguished between the Sabbath
and the Lord's Day (like Quakers,
preferring this name to Sunday). They
have emphasised the sacred character
of the Lord's Day, and the obligation
of Christians to celebrate the central act
of Christian worship—the Lord's Supper ;
but they have never been under any
delusion as to its being the " Christian
Sabbath." They have regarded such a
phrase as a contradiction in terms.

[1] See St. Augustine, *De Catech. Rudibus*, c. 41. Dr. Knox, the
late Bishop of Manchester, is surely wrong when he claims (*Pastors
and Teachers*, p. 82) that the ten commandments ever had equal
authority with the Lord's Prayer and the Apostles' Creed since
earliest times. For the opposite view see Dr. Gore, *Christian
Moral Principles*, p. 110. We are glad to note to-day, both in England,
Scotland, and America, a strong movement within the Episcopal
Church for the removal of the Ten Commandments from the Liturgy, a
position which they have occupied only since the Middle Ages. The
following statement from the late Archbishop Wm. Temple is indicative
of this temper : " The Decalogue should be totally removed from the
instruction of children ; it is by no means a good formulation of the
Christian moral law. . . . Many chaplains in the war found that the
Seventh Commandment was a positive hindrance to the inculcation
of true purity ; men drew a distinction between the ideal and the
obligation, and pleaded, with manifest sincerity, that though they
had lapsed from perfect purity they ' had not broken God's law ' "
(*The Pilgrim*, January, 1926, p. 215).

(b) They have always emphasised the *progressive* character of revelation, and insisted on " rightly dividing the Word of truth," first into Old and New Testaments ; and then into various types of literature within each of these.

(c) They have always repudiated those arguments for Infant Baptism which are drawn from the supposed analogy between Baptism and circumcision.[1]

(d) They have been free from the attacks of such pseudo-Jewish theories as Anglo-Israelitism, and in general from millenarian tendencies of any kind.

(e) Whilst the Old Testament Scriptures have been held in highest reverence, and have formed part of the lections in the Churches' worship, yet the hymns and psalms sung have been free from those cruder elements of Jewish theology, which have so often disfigured hymnody, but which are now happily disappearing everywhere.

(f) From the beginning the Churches have been opposed to slavery, and in America, whilst other great communions, such as the Baptists and Methodists, sustained a real break, which has not yet been healed, in both cases Disciples remained undivided.

[1] Such arguments are, of course, now rarely advanced by modern scholars, but occasionally they are still met with, as *e.g.* in *Christianity in History*, by Dr. Bartlet, and in *The Church and the Sacraments*, by Principal Clow.

Chapter V

FAITH AND WORKS

The Lutheran doctrine of justification by faith, which was the answer of the reforming party to the Roman Church's doctrine of justification by works of merit, had its own peculiar dangers. In going back behind the Mediæval Church, which had in a large measure so stultified religion as to reduce it to a mere mechanical process of merit-making, Luther anchored himself to the writings of Augustine and found in the African saint a soul in tune with his own. And from Augustine he was driven back upon Paul. And so Protestant Christianity—at least in all its orthodox forms—has always been essentially Pauline. But there is no doubt that Luther so far misunderstood both Paul and Augustine as to over-emphasise certain elements in their theology, and to place them out of perspective with other elements. This was especially so in connection with the relationship between faith and works. Luther's natural revulsion against the Roman emphasis on works, led him to find in Augustine, and in Paul, the doctrine of *justification by faith alone*, and to regard the

Epistle of James, with its emphasis on works, as a " right strawy epistle." But if Luther had drunk a little deeper of his hero Paul, he would have found the same emphasis : " Work out your own salvation with fear and trembling ; for it is God which worketh in you."[1] This emphasis on faith in contrast to works was sure to issue in a one-sided attitude to life, as it did in the history of Protestantism. It resulted, in the eighteenth and nineteenth centuries, in thorough-going doctrines of salvation by *faith alone*. And, moreover, in exercising faith men were regarded as purely passive. They could in no sense actively co-operate with the gift of God. The doctrines of " waiting on God " and " wrestling for salvation," of suppressing the will and doing nothing, were often so prevalent in extreme Evangelical circles, that it was considered rank heresy to talk of salvation being conditioned by any attitude or activity of our own. The question of the Jews on the Day of Pentecost, " What must we *do* ? " would have received the answer, " *Do* nothing." Luther had said, " In his actings towards God, in things pertaining to salvation or damnation, man has no free will but is the captive, the subject, and the servant, either of the will of God, or of Satan,"[2] and the *Formula of Concord* definitley stated that " before man is illumined, converted, regenerated, and drawn by the Holy Spirit, he can no more operate, co-operate, or

[1] Phil. ii. 13.   [2] *De Servo Arbitrio.*

49

even make a beginning towards his conversion or regeneration with his own natural powers than can a stone, a tree, or a piece of clay."[1] This attitude perhaps finds its most complete expression in James Proctor's hymn.

> Doing is a deadly thing,
> Doing ends in death.

With our newer psychological knowledge we no longer see the violent contrast between faith and works which Luther saw, and with our newer critical equipment for interpreting the New Testament we no longer see the contradiction between Paul and James which was so obvious to Luther. So that the old Lutheran opposition between *faith* and *works* disappears in the light of psychology, as it was never really present in the New Testament documents. Paul and James are not really in opposition, though we may admit that James does not scale the religious heights reached by the greater Apostle. He is, however, right in looking to the will—the sphere of conduct—for the final test. Whatever we believe we accept as true, but in such a way that it compels action. There must be an intellectual attitude, but that attitude must function—activity is the real test; and about this, when we interpret them historically, there is no sort of disagreement between Paul on the one hand and James and John on the other; for it is clear (as Campbell pointed out)

[1] See also the *Westminster Confession*, Chapter VI.

that Paul's objection to *works* in his earlier epistles is an objection to the *works of the old Jewish law*, not to activity on the part of Christians or would-be Christians, and that the *faith* he advocates is a " faith which *worketh* by love."[1]

That in the work of salvation, both in its initial stages and throughout life, man is called upon to *co-operate* with God there is now, I think, no kind of doubt in the minds of thinking Christians ; though amongst some sections of ultra-Evangelicals one may still hear the opposite maintained. The conviction, which we now all feel, I may best state in some words I once heard the late Dr. Selbie utter in the course of some lectures on the Atonement, " In making good the work of salvation the sinner himself has a share. The work is initiated by Jesus Christ, but cannot be completed without co-operation of those for whom He died. One of the great differences between the New Testament treatment of the subject and that which has often obtained in the Church, is that in the latter case men have been treated as merely passive recipients of benefit, whereas in the former they are always regarded as active participators in the transaction."

This had been stressed by Socinians and Quakers in the seventeenth and eighteenth centuries, and the early nineteenth century reformers took it up and *stressed it with added*

[1] Gal. v. 6.

force ; not only in connection with their doctrine of conversion, as we shall see in the next chapter, but also in connection with the Christian life to be lived. Thus they repudiated the narrow individualism of their day and emphasised the social aspects of Christianity.[1] Moreover, they

[1] Of course on the theological side this is the old controversy between Augustinianism and Pelagianism. The exaggerated form in which Augustinianism became prevalent in the Calvinistic theology, practically made God solely responsible for the eternal destruction of millions of the non-elect. It was thoroughly deterministic. In the process called conversion, the free-will of man was practically non-existent. Campbell was shocked beyond measure with this form of Calvinism, with which he came in contact. On the other hand Arminianism, though it rejected predestination, was largely Augustinian in the sense that it denied mans' part in salvation. I am aware that the late Prof. Platt maintains that Arminianism was Semi-Pelagian, but as I have maintained elsewhere, I am still convinced that in a very real sense it was Augustinian, and I find Harnack holds this view (see Platt's article in the *Encyclopædia of Religion and Ethics,* and Harnack, *History of Dogma.* See also Williston Walker's *History of the Christian Church,* p. 455). In the form in which Arminianism so often presented itself in the early nineteenth century, it was maintained that men must *wait* until the Holy Spirit moved them—virtually that they of themselves could do nothing. With his incisive mind Campbell saw again that this made God responsible for all who were lost, and in the New Testament he found nothing to justify this. So he and his co-workers, as those who have followed in their footsteps have always done, maintained that men must co-operate with God in winning the salvation which is offered. In *belief* the intellect must be *active* and not *passive,* and *faith* was not a matter of intellect alone, but personal *trust* carrying with it *loyalty,* which can only manifest itself in a loving *active* obedience to the will of God in Christ Jesus. They found that the New Testament called upon men to " save themselves," indicating clearly that while salvation was a free gift of God, yet man was called upon to play his part. Of course they were accused of being Pelagians and of denying the doctrine of grace ; accusations which were entirely false. They were in no sense Pelagian, if we understand by that term what is usually understood by it. They were Semi-Pelagians in the sense that they held a synergistic doctrine of grace—the active co-operation of the will of man with the free grace of God.

Calvinism of that day also stressed the doctrine of " once in grace always in grace." The elect could not fall. Nothing depended on

avoided in a large measure the tendency to separate religion from life and from morality,[1] so that in Churches of Christ in general, while there has been no lack of emphasis on the reverence due to God, on His free grace with which men may co-operate, there has been little of that false sentimentalism and sanctimonious unctuousness, which is sometimes mistaken for real piety. The Churches have also been free from emphasis on those grosser substitution theories of the Atonement, which have never altogether died out, and to-day are being revived again in some quarters of the religious world. On the other hand, the danger has been, in Churches of Christ, to lean too heavily on

their will. It is easy to see the danger of this doctrine from the ethical point of view, and this Campbell saw very clearly. His clear insight into the Pauline attitude to the Law of Moses, which we have noted in the previous chapter, prevented him from falling into the common error of exegesis, and interpreting Paul in Galatians and Romans as fulminating against Christian works of conduct. His method of collecting together all the material on any given subject, led him to place an equal emphasis on later Pauline statements, such as " they that believed in God might be careful to maintain good works." And he grasped the essential truth, that faith is concerned with *action* even more than with *belief*. This position has been maintained by Churches of Christ throughout their history, until to-day it is receiving confirmation from many quarters where once it was opposed.

[1] They would cordially have agreed with Prebendary Phillips, who, writing in the Anglo-Catholic Congress books, says, " The faith which is important in religion is an operative belief, a belief which leads to action. . . . But the faith on which St. Paul lays stress is more even than belief issuing in action, it is belief issuing in attraction. The devils, as St. James says, believe, and their belief leads to action, but the action consists in repulsion. . . . It is not merely belief which is necessary for us and not merely a faith which worketh, but ' a faith which worketh by love.' In one word it is trust."

moralism and to neglect those elements of personal communion with God which are such an essential part of the framework of early Christianity. But of this danger the Churches to-day are fully aware, and the balance is now being adjusted.

CHAPTER VI

THE DOCTRINE OF CONVERSION

HERE we are to deal with what is, I feel, the greatest contribution Churches of Christ have made to religious thought. In their doctrine of conversion—bound up as it is with the doctrine of Baptism—we have that which divides them from all other organised Christian bodies; on the one hand from Catholics and on the other from Protestants. It is true, however, that many individuals both amongst Catholics and Protestants are coming to see the truth of this doctrine, to which Churches of Christ have clung tenaciously from the beginning of the Movement. However much they may have differed on minor points, they have been united here. Although, like Baptists, they practise immersion and reject Infant Baptism, their *doctrine* of Baptism, and their teaching about its connection with conversion and regeneration, separate them from all other immersionists. Indeed, it is much more like the doctrine of Baptism which has been accepted in the Catholic Church from the earliest ages; for if members of

Churches of Christ accept anything, they certainly accept the affirmation of the Nicene Creed, " We believe in one Baptism *for the remission of sins.*" And as the Anglican Catechism professes, they firmly believe that *faith* and *repentance* are necessary pre-requisites to Baptism ; but unlike all the Catholic Churches— Anglican, Roman, and Eastern—they do not allow that faith and repentance can be exercised by proxy. They therefore reject Infant Baptism ; first because historically it had no part in the original Christian System, and secondly, because it violates that principle of Christ's religion which demands personal choice on the part of all His followers.

As we have seen, in the eighteenth century, emotionalism and enthusiasm were very much despised. But at the beginning of the nineteenth, conversion was a very popular thing amongst many Protestants ; but it was largely a matter of *feeling* and altogether subjective in character. Revivalism of a very wild type was very prevalent, and everywhere men declared they had " got religion." Emotionalism was the key-note of most preaching, and men and women were " converted " without any element of intellect or will entering into the process at all. Baptism was practised by Baptists, but it had no relationship to conversion, regeneration, or salvation. These things were altogether *mystical ;* by which was meant, not what we should mean by the term, but that they were conditioned solely by a deep emotional disturbance. Against all this Campbell, who looked at things very much from a rational point of view and who was a stern moralist, reacted with a doctrine of conversion which was eminently sane, and which with marvellously clear insight he built up from an exegesis of the New Testament documents.[1] And this doctrine Churches of Christ have preached throughout their history. Here and there the emotional element in conversion has been undervalued, even to the extent of denying to *feeling* any place at all. To deny any place to the feeling element is, of course, an exaggeration of the position taken up by the pioneers, neither is it possible in view of psychological investigation into religion nor of historical investigation into the beginnings of Christianity. But an unrestrained emotional element in religion, divorced from elements of intellect and will, has always proved disastrous. And this Campbell and others saw clearly enough. They recognised that conversion had to do with the whole man— with the intellect, the emotions, and the will. And so, from their study of the New Testament, they proclaimed that salvation was *conditioned* by the free *co-operation* of the individual. Whilst it was in the fullest sense the gift of God, yet they proclaimed, against both Calvinism and Arminianism, that man was a *free agent* in accepting Christ as his Saviour.

[1] See his Essays on *Remission of Sins*, and *Regeneration*.

They saw clearly enough that in the process of conversion three things were involved in man's co-operation—faith, repentance, and Baptism. As to faith, it was conditioned by *belief*, a definite intellectual element, but it was more than mere belief—it was trust in, and loyalty to the Person of our Lord Jesus Christ. Thus it always involved an *active* element leading to complete obedience to the will of Jesus as Lord. As to repentance, it was more than a mere stirring of the emotions—a matter of sorrow. It too involved a definite *active* element. And so Campbell laid great stress on what he called *reformation* as the chief element in repentance. It would necessarily be conditioned by the emotions, but it was not to end there. It was a complete turning round—a change of view resulting in a change of life. As to Baptism, it was *not a mere obedience* to the arbitrary will of Christ, neither did it simply admit into some local or universal society. It did this, for it admitted the baptised into the Body of Christ, the Church of the living God, which was the sphere of salvation, and normally of the Holy Spirit's operations. But it was also *in order to the remission of sins and the gift of the Holy Spirit* : it was a burial with Christ and a resurrection in the likeness of His resurrection ; it was the birth of water spoken of in John's Gospel, and as such, was indeed the " bath of regeneration." It was the first *act*, signifying the complete surrender of the whole being to Jesus Christ as Lord, and as such was to be followed by a whole life of active obedience to His will. It translated a man into a new relationship to the Godhead— changed his state—and introduced him into the sphere of grace—the Divine Society.

Of course when this teaching was preached it raised a terrific storm. The reformers were accused of being "papists."[1] But Campbell responded that if this was "papacy," it was also good New Testament doctrine, and they could well claim, that whilst the doctrine might be that of Catholic Christianity in general, as they proceeded to show that it was, quoting copiously from the Fathers, yet it was so with a difference, for the Baptism which was unto the remission of sins was that of sincere penitent believers.[2]

---

[1] In those days little was known of Catholicism outside the Roman Church.

[2] Of course this *doctrine* of Baptism, for which Churches of Christ. plead, is essentially the Catholic doctrine, as it is of course that of the Protestant Confessions ; though Protestantism has generally rejected it, regarding Baptism as a bodily act which signifies something already accomplished, rather than an act which effects something Churches of Christ differ from Catholics in general as to the *subjects* of Baptism, and from Western Catholics as to the administration of Baptism, regarding, as Eastern Catholics do, *immersion* as the valid form ; but as to *doctrine* they hold the essentially Catholic doctrine, because it is also the doctrine of the Apostolic Church, and moreover it is psychologically sound. (See an article I contributed to *The Interpreter*, April, 1924, on *Baptism and Psychology*.) Alexander Campbell would have agreed heartily with a good deal of what is said by Fr. Thornton in the four paragraphs on pp. 9 to 12 of the Green Book on Baptism published by the Anglo-Catholic Congress. I may be allowed to refer the reader for a fuller discussion of this matter to what I have written in Chapter IX of *Essays on Christian Unity*. Of this chapter *The Pilgrim* very kindly said, "Yet even on the subject of Conversion and its relation to Baptism, where he argues strongly for the restriction of Baptism to adult persons, he advances no theory for which room could not be

That Infant Baptism arose late in the second century and did not become universal until Augustine emphasised his doctrine of original *sin* (or original *guilt*, as we should prefer to call it) with its corollary of the damnation of infants dying unbaptised, is now generally admitted by competent scholars of all schools.[1] Campbell took up this position and also denied that Augustine's theory of original guilt, carrying with it as it necessarily did the damnation of unbaptized infants, was to be found in the New Testament. This was a strong position to take up in those days, but we may claim that it has been thoroughly justified by Modern New Testament exegesis, and by modern psychology. As Mr. Moxon says, " It is now generally felt that Augustine's view of the guilt of Original Sin

found in a reunited and Catholic Church." See further, *Conversion to God*, by Alex. Brown, and *Small Books on New Testament Christianity*, No. 5, by W. Mander, B.A.

[1] The late Prof. Gwatkin said, " We have good evidence that infant baptism is no direct institution either of the Lord himself or of his apostles. There is no trace of it in the New Testament " (*Early Church History*, Vol. I, p. 251). Williston Walker says, " The strong probability is that till past the middle of the second century persons baptised were those only of years of discretion " (*A History of the Christian Church*, p. 95). Harnack, speaking of the sub-Apostolic Age, says, " There is no sure trace of infant baptism in this epoch ; personal faith is a necessary condition " (*History of Dogma*, Vol. I, p. 208). Duchesne, the great Roman Catholic scholar, makes it quite clear in his *Christian Worship*, and his Church History, that Infant Baptism arose late and did not become universal till after Augustine's day. In this he follows the late Prof. Dollinger, who said in his *First Age of Christianity and the Church*, " There is no proof or hint in the New Testament that the Apostles baptised infants, or ordered them to be baptised " (p. 325). More recently infant Baptism has been questioned by Emil Brunner (see his *Encounter with God*), and by Karl Barth (see his *Die Kirchliche Lehre von der Taufe*). See also *Dr. Whale and Infant Baptism*, by James Gray, M.A.

involves a contradiction in terms, and on the face of it stands self-condemned. Guilt is only predicable of the individual's wilful act."[1] He further goes on to say, " Augustine admits that sin springs from the will, yet he asserts that it is for inherited sin that man will be lost. This implies that Original Sin is to be accounted more serious than wilful sin—a view which is in conflict with all sane judgment . . . . *Original Sin is a feature of Augustinianism that is a shocking travesty of the Catholic Faith.*"[2] Psychologists are agreed that the moral sense does not function in any real way until the dawn of adolescence. Not till then is there any real sense of sin. Conversion is then possible, and hence Baptism for the remission of sins may be administered. It ought, of course, to be remembered that the age at which this takes place will vary with different children. With some it may be as early as the age of ten, and more frequently as early as twelve.

That Paul, far from teaching the doctrine of justification by faith *alone*, held a very high doctrine of Baptism, that he was in a certain sense what is now called a sacramentalist, is now also widely admitted by modern Protestant scholars. It used to be the fashion to think of Paul as placing little or no value on Baptism, but it is now seen by modern scholars that this

[1] *The Doctrine of Sin*, p. 93.
[2] *Ibid.*, p. 106. See further the fuller treatment in N. P. Williams' Bampton Lectures, *The Ideas of the Fall and of Original Sin.*

position is historically unsound.[1] But over a
century ago Campbell and Scott, both reared
in the Protestant world, saw this quite clearly.
They claimed, and Churches of Christ have ever
claimed, that " Baptism is the grave of the old
man, and the birth of the new. As he sinks
beneath the baptismal waters, the believer buries
there all his corrupt affections and past sins ;
as he emerges thence, he rises regenerate,
quickened to new hopes and a new life."[2]

[1] See the article originally contributed to *The Expositor* by
Prof. Andrews, and now included in Dr. Forsyth's book, *The Church
and the Sacraments*. Prof. Andrews sums up by saying, " It seems
very hard to resist the conclusion (however little we may like it) that
if the Epistles of St. Paul do not enunciate the ecclesiastical doctrine
of Baptismal Regeneration—they at any rate approximate very
closely to it—with this difference, of course, that there is no shred
of real proof that baptism was ever administered to infants in the
Apostolic Age." So Prof. E. F. Scott has recently said, " For
Paul then, baptism marks the moment in which the Spirit is vouch-
safed to the believer, and as such it has a twofold import. (1) On
the one hand it cleanses from sin and effects the renewal which is
the necessary condition of the higher life. . . . (2) On the other
hand, as he undergoes a change within himself, so the convert is
united in baptism with the holy community " (*The Spirit in the
New Testmanet*, p. 154). So Prof. Underwood has recently written,
" The merely symbolic view of baptism does not do justice to the
Apostle's phrases about ' putting on Christ,' ' dying to sin,' and
' being raised to newness of life,' in baptism. For Paul, baptism
means an experiential union with Christ in His redeeming acts "
(*Conversion : Christian, and Non-Christian*, p. 110). Principal
Wheeler Robinson in reviewing this book of Prof. Underwood's
in the *Baptist Times*, was thankful to note that the Zwinglian view
of the sacrament, to which Baptist Churches had adhered, was
rejected by Prof. Underwood. See further, Meyer and Heiler
amongst Continental scholars.

[2] Lightfoot, *Colossians*, p.182.

Chapter VII

CREEDS AND LIBERTY

WHILST Churches of Christ have, like Catholic Christianity in general, always placed great emphasis on the Church as a Divine Society, on Church unity, and on the sacraments of Baptism and the Lord's Supper as real channels of grace; yet they have differed significantly from Catholic Christianity in rejecting creeds and confessions and have regarded them as divisive in their influence. In this their attitude has been nearer to that of Quakers. It must not, however, be understood that they have been unconcerned about belief itself, regarding it as a matter of indifference what was believed. No! they have contended earnestly for the "faith once for all delivered to the saints," but they have ever been opposed to the summing up of that faith in a creed or confession, regarding the New Testament itself as a sufficient basis of union for all Christians. Moreover they have always been suspicious of *metaphysical explanations* of the facts of Christianity, and have refused to make them binding upon men's consciences. Thus they have never regarded *theories* of inspiration, of the entrance of sin into the world, of predestination, of the Atonement, of the Incarnation, and the Trinity, as of the Faith. It was chiefly against the creeds and confessions of the sixteenth and seventeenth centuries—creeds which are full of such metaphysical explanations—that the early reformers protested. They declared that they themselves were neither Arminian nor Calvinistic, neither Unitarian nor Trinitarian but simply Christian; and they saw clearly enough that such confessions were divisive in their effects. Their attention seems not to have been directed at all to such a simple statement of *facts* as the Apostles' Creed. There is no doubt that they would have accepted every clause of it, but only because they could have found these clauses within the New Testament itself, and because they expressed the *facts* of the Faith and not abstract theological dogmas.

In the history of Churches of Christ, whilst there has been universal antipathy to a written creed, and to religious tests in *the form of confessions*, three distinct attitudes have emerged with regard to the Faith itself.

(a) It has often been urged that the New Testament itself is the creed. This has not been very successfully urged, because it is clear that the New Testament, in the strictest sense, is not a creed.

It is rather a collection of documents which, as Campbell claimed, must be interpreted historically.[1] But what has been meant by this claim has been that the New Testament must be the final court of appeal in settling matters of faith and order, and this is sound enough.

(b) It has been said that Christ Himself is the creed, and that Christians are called upon, not to believe in theories about Christ, but to believe in Christ Himself; not to believe in a creed, but in a Person. This is really involved in the emphasis which Churches of Christ have always placed on *faith* as *trust* in a Person and *loyalty* to Him.[2] Of course it is, strictly speaking, impossible to believe *in* Christ without believing something *about* Him, but this attitude has witnessed to the important truth that the first essential of Christian life is faith *in* Jesus Christ as a Person, and not the acceptance of a series of dogmas, many of them conditioned by most subtle metaphysics, often quite out-worn.

---

[1] See a series of articles in the *Christian Advocate* by Joseph Smith, beginning with the issue for May 20, 1921. See further, *Should Creeds be Mended or Ended?* by J. B. Rotherham.

[2] Cf. *Grace and Personality,* by Principal Oman, where he urges that our relationship to God is simply " trust in a person whose whole dealing with us proves Him worthy of trust " (p. 75). No greater work could be read on the subject of grace than this book which has recently been re-issued in an enlarged form.

(c) Quite generally amongst Churches of Christ, it has been urged that the simple baptismal confessions of the New Testament are the only written creeds which ought to be imposed on any candidate for admission to the Church. The earliest baptismal confession seems to have been, " I believe that Jesus is Lord."[1] The passage which at a later date found its way into the Acts of the Apostles, " I believe that Jesus is the Christ the Son of the living God," bears witness to the fact that this creed was early used *as a definite baptismal confession*,[2] as does also the statement at the close of the Fourth Gospel.[3]

It has been this latter creed, associated as it is with Peter's Confession at Cæsarea Philippi,[4] which Churches of Christ have made central.[5]

[1] See Acts of the Apostles, and Rom. x. 9. In this passage the open confession seems also to be coupled with belief in the resurrection of Jesus.

[2] See Acts viii. 37, A.V.

[3] John xx. 31.

[4] See Matt. xvi. 16 ; Luke ix. 20 ; Mark viii. 29. Of course as used by Peter this is not a confession of Deity as we understand it. It is merely a confession of Messiahship. [Note Luke's account, " Thou art the Christ (Messiah) of God."] But as used in the Fourth Gospel, and in the interpolated passage in Acts, it is clearly more than this. It is in the fullest sense a confession of the Deity of our Lord. It is in this full sense that Churches of Christ have ever used it as a baptismal confession.

[5] I have found one document giving the fuller confession as stated by Paul in 1 Cor. xv. 3-5. (1) That Christ died for our Sins ; (2) that He was buried ; (3) that He rose again the third day (see the Trust Deed of the Rodney Street Church, Wigan, 1860). Meyer thinks this may well have been the baptismal Confession on which Paul was admitted to the Church in Damascus. See *The Christian Advocate*, June 26, 1925.

The early reformers recognised, as modern New Testament scholars have since done, that here was a crucial moment in the ministry of our Lord, and that in Peter's confession was the important summing up of the Christian Faith, and so they made this the only Confession of Faith *necessary for those demanding Baptism*, just as the Apostles' Creed at a late date became the baptismal confession of the Western Church. It is customary in Churches of Christ for this Confession to be made audibly, before witnesses, by every candidate for Baptism.[1]

So strong has been the feeling in Churches of Christ against producing any elaborate statement of belief, which might be made binding upon members as a creed and provide the basis of a heresy charge, that there has always been a distinct aversion to producing formularies of any kind. Whenever formularies have had to be produced the preamble has always stated that they are in no sense to be taken as a creed binding on all future generations.[2] The same applies to many tracts and books published.

This attitude towards creeds has produced that necessary liberty within the Church of Christ which is essential to its growth. There has been a remarkable absence of heresy-hunts, and room for growth and expansion. It might be thought that such liberty would develop into

[1] See 1 Tim. vi. 12. See a statement I made at the *Geneva Conference*, 1920, p. 66 of the report.
[2] See the Formularies presented to the Geneva Conference, 1920.

licence, but the history of Churches of Christ has not proved this to be the case. They have found that in things essential there has been unity, whilst they have allowed the fullest liberty of opinion in things doubtful, endeavouring to exercise charity in all things. They have maintained a remarkable corporate unity without either a highly organised ecclesiastical polity, or a written confession of faith, apart from the baptismal confession which makes the Person of Jesus Christ central. That in this they have been helped by their emphasis on Baptism and the Lord's Supper, their loyalty to these two sacraments and to the idea of the One Body, there can be little doubt.[1]

[1] It is pleasing to find the position taken up by Churches of Christ with regard to the centrality of the Person of Jesus, and their emphasis on the baptismal confession, being advocated in many quarters. See a suggestive paper by Mr. Nowell Smith, M.A., on *The Centrality of Jesus*, in the *Modern Churchman*, September, 1921. In the same number Canon T. H. Bindley asks the question, " Would not a confession of personal devotion to our Lord Jesus Christ as Supreme Revealer of the Love of God, and as Saviour of the world, suffice ? " He argues for this, pp. 310-314. Dr. Cyril Norwood, Headmaster of Harrow, says, " The Eunuch asked Philip : ' What doth hinder me to be baptised ? ' and Philip said : ' If thou believest thou mayest.' And he answered and said : ' I believe that Jesus Christ is the Son of God.' Is there any evidence that more than this simple affirmation was required in those first days ? I cannot find that more was required " (p. 322). See also Principal Jacks, *Religious Perplexities*. Further, see *The Church and the Creeds*, by Daniel Lamont, pp. 16 and 17, Bishop Lawrence of the American Episcopal Church, in his recent book, *Fifty Years*, tells how he asked in the House of Bishops, " What right has any branch of the Catholic Church to set up a bar of entrance to the Church which is higher than that used by the Apostles themselves ? " and how he heard the Bishop of Southern Ohio plead that the baptismal creed should be, " I believe in the Lord Jesus Christ, the Son of God." Again he touches the root of the matter when he asks, " Do we not make a mistake in thinking that the Creeds are our chief instruments in binding us together in unity ? "

Chapter VIII

EMPHASIS ON CORPORATE UNITY

As we have seen, the Movement we are considering arose out of what may well be called a *passion for Christian Unity*, and this passion has never been lost. As Mr. H. E. Tickle, one of the representatives of the British Churches to the Geneva Conference, said, " The advocacy of the union of all believers is largely the justification for the separate existence of the Churches of Christ."[1] This passion for unity has been witnessed to by constant preaching and by masses of literature which the Movement has produced.[2] The method advocated was a *restoration* of the essentials of faith, order, and discipline of Apostolic Christianity ; but the main emphasis—the central message—has ever been the union of all Christians in one corporate society.

From the beginning, the Movement recognised that in the New Testament there is one Body—

[1] Report, p. 50.
[2] See *St. Paul on Christian Unity*, by J. B. Cowden ; *That They may All be One* ; *The Herald of Unity*, published for a number of years by Mr. Jno. M'Cartney, etc.

the Church of Christ—just as there is one Lord, one Faith, and one Baptism. The Pauline doctrine of the Body of Christ has always been strongly emphasised, as has also the high priestly prayer of our Lord in John xvii., " that they all may be one."

Thus Churches of Christ have differed in several respects from the normal Protestant emphasis, and have leaned more towards the Catholic emphasis, though with a difference. (1) They have always denied the doctrine of the *invisible Church*, in the sense that Christ's institution was not meant to have a definite visible organisation on earth. They have seen clearly, what is now generally recognised, that this doctrine is not found in the New Testament and have waived it aside as a subtlety which does not really get rid of the difficulty of the existing state of division in Christendom. (2) They have never been individualistic in their attitude to salvation, but have recognised that in the New Testament *salvation is related to the corporate society*, with its visible corporate institutions such as Baptism, the Lord's Supper, discipline, etc. They have consistently taught and preached a very high doctrine of the Church as the Divine Society.[1]   (3) They have rejected

[1] To illustrate this I may quote from *Struggles and Triumphs of the Truth*, a work published in 1888 by Prof. Lowber, D.Sc., Ph.D., a distinguished member of the Movement in America.   On p. 171 he says, " There is a tendency among Protestants to disregard the authority of the Church, and to look upon it simply as a moral society.   The ' Disciples ' believe the Church divine, and that

the *branch theory* of the Church, by which different denominations are regarded as branches of the one vine. Historically this is quite an inaccurate exegesis of John xv. ; for the branches are the individual members of the Church, not competing denominations. This branch theory has sometimes been advocated in the form of a *regiment theory*, the different denominations being regarded as regiments in the one army. But this breaks down, for every army is an organised unit, and it is obvious that in the present state of Christendom the different denominations are in no sense units of one visible organisation. As Canon Lacey has recently pointed out,[1] the idea of the Church is before that of the Churches, and the Churches themselves are local societies of the One Body, and not separate organisations. (4) They have consistently pleaded that *sectarianism is sin*, making a strong point of Paul's words in 1 Cor. i. and iii. ; that it is a state of things which is seriously hindering the advance of Christ's Kingdom. It is a sin in which we are all sharers to some

it is as important to obey the bride as the bridegroom. Hence they do not believe that a man can be a Christian out of the Church." See also *The Church*, by Mr. Joseph Smith. See further, *The Christian System*, Chapter XXIV, Campbell s Essay on *The Kingdom of Heaven*, and several essays on *The Nature of the Christian Organisation*, which he wrote for the *Millennial Harbinger*, and which subsequently were published in this country in the *Christian Messenger*. Campbell, writing of the Body of Christ, says, " Christians must regard the Church, or body of Christ, as one community, though composed of many small communities, each of which is an organised member of this great national organisation."

[1] *The One Body and the One Spirit.*

extent. (5) They have urged that methods of federation, exchange of pulpits, intercommunion, do not really touch the heart of the matter of division, and that the only solution is *organic unity*. This, they have pleaded, can only come by study, discussion, and conference, assisted by serious prayer for the healing of the schisms in the seamless robe of Christ. We must be real, and face the difficulties. We must ask, What is Christ's intention for His institution ? and be ready to follow the guidance of His will.

Further, from the beginning of the Movement, the abandonment of all sectarian names has been urged, and the adoption advocated of such scriptural and catholic names as Churches of Christ, Christian, Disciple. Churches of Christ have often been misunderstood with regard to these names. It has been thought that they adopted them in a spirit of arrogance, but nothing has been further from their thoughts. They have always felt, as did Paul, when writing to Corinth, that party names are the backbone of partyism, and have desired to be known only by the name of Christ, Whom they have sought to follow.

The ideal of the Church universal has not always been maintained at the same level amongst Churches of Christ, and this largely because they have always desired to witness to what is equally apostolic—the autonomy of the Church in each locality. And we may rejoice that, even amongst Episcopal Churches to-day, there is a growing recognition of this need. There has very rightly been a fear of over-stressed ecclesiastical organisation, and this has sometimes led to a lack of hope in an *organised* universal Church. It has in fact been argued by some that the universal Church can only be spoken of in the same sense that we speak of the English Jury—a body which has no real existence. But this is obviously inadequate to the New Testament conception. From the beginning, however, stress has been laid upon co-operation, and on the fact that Christ's Church on earth should be visibly one as it was in the first age,[1] and this is the message which

---

[1] Speaking of the Catholic Epistles in the New Testament Campbell said, " The very basis of such general or universal letters is the fact, that all the communities of Christ constitute but one body, and are individually and mutually bound to co-operate in all things pertaining to a common salvation " (*Christian System*, p. 77). Writing against any form of absolute independency he said, " All societies demonstrate in their history, not merely a tendency to centralisation, but the necessity of a general superintendency of some sort, without which the conservative principle cannot operate to the prosperity and furtherance of the public interests of the community. But the New Testament itself teaches both by precept and example the necessity of united and concentrated action in the advancement of the Kingdom. . . . It indicates, (1) the necessity of co-operation, (2) the necessity of two distinct classes of officers in every particular community, (3) the necessity of a third class of public functionaries [Evangelists], (4) the utility and the need for special deliberations, and of conventions on peculiar emergencies, (5) It allows not persons to send themselves or to ordain themselves to office ; but everywhere intimates the necessity of choice, selection, mission, and ordination . . . (7) It claims for every functionary the concurrence of those portions of the community in which he labours, and holds him responsible to those who send, appoint, or ordain him to office " (*Christian Messenger*, Vol. VI, p. 160).

Churches of Christ urge upon the religious world to-day.

It should be remembered that when the Movement began, there was an almost total lack of desire for Christian Unity. Divisions were justified by all parties in the Protestant world, and as we have seen, not only divisions, but sheer individualism. Campbell was a far-seeing man. He not only saw that *the Church occupied the central position* in the New Testament, and that the Church was one, but as a philosopher he realised that man was a social animal and *needed a society* or divine fellowship in which to realise salvation.[1]

To-day the Body of Christ is grievously wounded and its unity impaired, but we may rejoice that the ideal, which Churches of Christ have ever held before the world, is now a message on the lips of nearly all Christians. There is a passionate longing for some form of visible unity, witnessed to by any number of different movements and societies. Our prayer is that the Church may be guided to a unity *in harmony with the will of Christ*, a unity which will be permanent, and not one which will sow the seeds of future division. Such a unity will need to relate itself to those visible marks of the Church's unity which characterised the Apostolic Church —the one Faith, the ordinances of Baptism and

---

[1] In this he anticipated a good deal of what was later advanced by Josiah Royce, and like Loisy and Tyrrell, he taught that " religion was made for man and not man for religion."

the Lord's Supper, and the divinely appointed ministry. It will further need to reduce ecclesiastical organisation to the lowest minimum necessary for the expression of its unity, and above all to be based upon a free fellowship in love. The task is tremendously difficult, but there are many hopeful signs that a better day is dawning.[1]

[1] The formation of the British Council of Churches in 1942 and the World Council of Churches is a sign full of hope.

Chapter IX

CHURCH ORDER

It cannot be said that Churches of Christ have always maintained the same emphasis on Church order as on the sacraments. But from the beginning it was not so.

In the beginning of the Movement, stress was laid upon the New Testament order of ministry. It was clearly recognised that in the New Testament Church there was both a temporary or extraordinary ministry, and a permanent or ordinary ministry. The early reformers urged that a regular and constant ministry was needed by the Church, and that such ministry *was of divine authority*. But the Movement was a reaction against *professionalism* in the ministry, and if Butler is any sure witness to the state of the clergy in the early eighteenth century, such a reaction was indeed needed. This antipathy to *professionalism* remains a characteristic of Churches of Christ. They are always ready to adopt safeguards against it. Then, too, the Movement reacted against what was called " one man ministry," in which the whole worship of a congregation, with the exception of a little singing, was carried on by one man. It was clear that, in the New Testament Church, there was a plurality of Presbyters (Elders), who ministered in the congregation, to say nothing of Deacons and lower orders, who were needed for the performance of sacred duties. Moreover, the Churches have always witnessed to what they have called " mutual ministry," that is, the right of all, who are duly qualified and gifted, to read, pray, and preach in the worship of the Church, even though they are not called and ordained to the sacred offices of Presbyter or Deacon. And they have refused to make that rigid distinction between *clergy* and *laity*, which has so characterised most Churches. To this end ministers of Churches of Christ of whatever order *do not style themselves " reverend."* The Churches rejoice that others, especially the Society of Friends, have witnessed to similar things.

That these general principles have been exaggerated in the course of the Churches' history, no one would deny.[1] But such exaggerations of good and sound principles have been abnormal, much as Montanism was in the early Church, and to-day are not at all characteristic of the general body of Churches of Christ.

The Churches recognise three major orders as belonging to the permanent ministry of the

---

[1] See *Memoirs of David King;* also *Christian Ministry*, by J. B. Rotherham. As early as 1843 Campbell strongly protested against such exaggeration, which had crept into the Churches, and which he vividly describes (*Christian Messenger*, Vol. VII, p. 114).

Church : Evangelists or Missionaries, Bishops or Presbyters, and Deacons.

Evangelists are not officers of the local Church, but of the Church universal in any given locality, city, district, state, county, or country. They are Missionaries who are sent out to bring Churches into being by preaching the Gospel, and having brought them into being, to exercise temporary jurisdiction over them, and finally organise them with their own Bishops and Deacons. They may also be called to work with weak and struggling Churches in need of help. Their chief work is to convert men and women by the power of the Gospel. These Evangelists are wholly supported and set apart to this sacred work, and to-day both in America, Australia, New Zealand and Great Britain they are trained in theological colleges ; though a man might be called to office without such training, were he competent and qualified.

Presbyters and Bishops are identified as one, and are officers called and ordained to rule in local congregations. Their work is to rule, administer discipline, to teach the elements of the Christian Faith, and to administer the Lord's Supper.[1] They " watch for the souls of the

---

[1] Teaching is not confined to the Presbyters, but they are responsible that the flock is taught and admonished in Christian faith and conduct. The Lord's Supper, it is generally allowed, may be administered by others than Presbyters in Churches which are not fully organised, and similarly under the direction of the Presbyters in fully organised Churches ; but Presbyters, in such fully organised Churches, are the normal officers of its administration.

congregation as those who must give an account."[1] In some cases Presbyters are supported, and in others partly supported. On the other hand they are usually quite unsupported by the Church.

Deacons are appointed and ordained to watch over temporalities in the Church, and to assist the Presbyters in the varied ministry.

Churches of Christ have always strenuously resisted forms of sacerdotalism. The power of ordination is within the Church itself, which is the priestly body ; it does not reside in any particular individual or class. In reality it is Christ Himself Who ordains, baptises, and dispenses the Supper, not any priestly body.[2] This does not mean, however, that the congregations rule the Presbyters, for as Campbell claimed, " Whatever rights, duties, or privileges are conferred on particular persons, cannot of right belong to those who have transferred them ; any more than a person cannot both give and keep the same thing."[3] The authority of the Presbyters to rule in the Church is clearly outlined in the New Testament epistles, but the law of Christ's Kingdom is *love*, and so is the guiding principle of this rule and authority vested in the sacred ministry. But the rights of the congregation in selection and ordination are also clear, and to this Churches of Christ have

[1] Heb. xiii. 17.
[2] To this all the ancient liturgies witness.
[3] *Christian System*, p. 81.

witnessed. To-day we may rejoice that even leading Episcopalians are concerned that their Church has lost this right, and are seeking to restore it.[1]

Needless to say Churches of Christ, with their high doctrine of the Church, have always opposed State establishment.

Finally, one cannot close this chapter without paying a tribute of praise to hundreds of unselfish souls in the Churches, who in each generation, besides following their ordinary daily work, have spent themselves, in season and out of season, in proclaiming Christ as the Saviour of the world and Lord of His Church. In this respect Churches of Christ have a long record of noble and devoted service.

[1] See Dr. Gore, *The Holy Spirit and the Church*. See further the Report of the Commission on Ordination presented to the Conference of the British Churches in 1942.

CHAPTER X

BAPTISM AND THE LORD'S SUPPER

ONE of the distinguishing marks of Churches of Christ is the position they have assigned to the sacraments of the Church (or as they have generally preferred to call them, using the language of a section of the Protestant world of the early nineteenth century—the ordinances). They have seen, from the earliest days of the Movement, as clearly as Professor Andrews, Bousset, Kirsopp Lake, Meyer, and Heiler have since pointed out, that the Christianity of Paul and the early Church was an *institutional religion*. In 1843 Campbell, describing the Movement, could say, " The current reformation, *if conspicuous now or hereafter* for anything, must be so because of the conspicuity it gives the Bible and its ordinances as the *indispensable moral means of spiritual life and health* . . . . . The distinguishing characteristic is *a restoration of the ordinances of the new institution to their place and power*."[1]   He even classed the Bible itself as one of the ordinances of the Church ; and described

[1] *Christian Messenger*, Vol. VII, p. 39.

an ordinance as " the mode in which the grace of God acts on human nature." Earlier, in 1835, he had written, " In the Kingdom of Heaven, faith is then the *principle*, and ordinances the *means*, of enjoyment, because all the wisdom, power, love, mercy, compassion, or *grace of God* is in the ordinances of the Kingdom of Heaven ; and if all grace be in them, it can only be enjoyed through them. What then . . . are the ordinances which contain the grace of God ? They are preaching the Gospel—immersion in the name of Jesus into the name of the Father, and of the Son, and of the Holy Spirit—the reading and teaching of the Living Orackes—the Lord's day—the Lord's supper—fasting—prayer—confession of sins— and praise."[1]

Further, it will be seen that there has been no question of limiting the ordinances to two in number ; though Baptism and the Lord's Supper have ever been placed central as the two great institutions of the Church.[2]

The question of Baptism we have already discussed in the chapter on Conversion, and we have seen how the early pioneers differed from

[1] *Christian System*, p. 174. From a philosophical point of view, Campbell also saw quite clearly that the Incarnation—the central doctrine of Christianity—was carried forward, in principle, in the Church and the ordinances. He rejected the accusation that Baptism was a mere external bodily act, and claimed that it was an act of the whole man, but recognised that, in our present state, body and spirit are so closely related, that bodily acts are a necessary means for the conveyance of spiritual grace. See *Christian System*, p. 246.

[2] On this point see also *The Scheme of Redemption*, by Dr. Milligan, and Appendix A of this book.

the Scotch Baptists (McLeanists) and from the General Baptists, in their view of the design or doctrine of Baptism, whilst they agreed with them as to the subjects and the act.[1] We may therefore pass on to deal with the Lord's Supper.

Long before the Catholic revival in the Anglican Church had emphasised the Lord's Supper as the central act of worship, the Glasites in the eighteenth century had done the same thing in their communities. They had renounced the over-emphasis on preaching to which Presbyterianism had witnessed, and restored the Lord's Supper, with its quiet reverence, its accompaniments of prayer, praise, and reading the Sacred Word, to its primitive position as the centre of the Church's corporate worship. And this emphasis was carried on by

---

[1] Their teaching that Baptism was " for the remission of sins," they justified by an historical exegesis of the New Testament documents, an exegesis which modern scholarship has more than justified, especially with regard to Paul. See in this connection *Jesus and Paul,* by Dr. Bacon, who says, " Christianity was to Paul the Way of justification or peace with God which he saw symbolised in the two primitive observances of baptism and the supper. . . . Christianity consisted in the ordinances and their interpretation." See also Heiler, *Der Catholizismus;* Dr. Angus, *Christianity and the Mystery Religions;* Wilfred Knox, *St. Paul and the Jerusalem Church.* But they also used pragmatic arguments much in the same way that Loisy does in *The Gospel and the Church.* In later years the arguments offered were often of a very rigid logical type, and some members of the Churches undoubtedly felt the strain of this. To-day, however, an apologetic based on modern scholarship—on historical exegesis of the New Testament, and on psychology—is being put forward. See *Conversion,* by W. Mander, B.A. Suffice it to say that Churches of Christ have ever been held together by their adherence to the Apostolic doctrine of the relationship of Baptism to regeneration, to conversion, to the remission of sins, and to the gift of the Holy Spirit.

the Baptist Churches which had been influenced by McLean, from whom in this country Churches of Christ sprang into existence. The same emphasis characterised the work of Campbell and his followers in America. It is sometimes objected, that in Catholic Churches the emphasis on worship which centres in the Lord's Supper has led to degeneracy in preaching, and there is some justification for this. But Churches of Christ have provided an example, throughout their history, of making the Lord's Table central without such lack of recognition of the power of preaching ; for like the late Dr. Forsyth, the early nineteenth-century reformers made preaching an ordinance or sacrament.

With Churches of Christ, then, the chief service on every Lord's Day is the Lord's Supper ; and in such services the Lord's Table is centrally placed. It is in this service more than in any other that the Church, as a royal priesthood, offers worship to God through the great High Priest her Lord.[1] Baptism, self-examination,

---

[1] Campbell said on this head, " There is in the Christian temple a table, appropriately called the Lord's table, as a part of its furniture. . . . ' The cup of the Lord ' and ' the loaf ' for which thanks were continually offered, are the furniture of this table. . . . If it be shown that in the Lord's house there is the Lord's table, as a part of the furniture, it must always be there " (*Christian System*, p. 304). The pulpit has never been the central object of furniture in the Churches in this country. The centrality of the Lord's Supper has been symbolised by placing the Lord's Table central, usually on a raised platform at the end of the building. In America I believe the pulpit has in more recent years been placed central, but as in many Free Churches in this country, there is a decided movement in the American Churches away from this, and back to what was the original intention of the early reformers.

and an upright life have been regarded as the
necessary pre-requisites of all who celebrate
and partake.[1] Here we have Churches where
it is the normal habit of all the members to
communicate each Lord's Day. The Feast is
a service of obligation.

Great stress has always been placed on the
Lord's Supper as an *act of worship*, and on the
priestly character of the whole Church ; and in
this service those four elements which have
been characteristic of Christian worship throughout all ages find their place : (1) the reading of
the Gospels and the Apostolic writings,[2] usually
accompanied by instruction in the form of a
sermon at some part of the service ; (2) the
offering of gifts ; (3) prayers ; (4) the " breaking
of the bread."[3] To these has been added the

[1] The Churches in this country have ever been " close com-
munionists," but not in the sense of restricting communion to their
own members, but to the baptised. They have never intended by
this any reflection on the honesty of purpose, or sincerity of heart of
those, the validity of whose Baptism they could not accept, nor have
they in any way wished to place any limits on the operation of God's
grace ; but they have recognised the inconsistency of pleading for a
valid Baptism and then ignoring such a plea when it came to the
administration of Holy Communion. In America the case has been
somewhat different. From the very early days the difficulty was
overcome by adopting a policy of " neither inviting nor debarring "
from the Lord's Table. See further a reply to the F.C.F.C. published
in the *Christian Advocate*, June 22nd, 1945. More recently a practice
of " Guest Communion " has been adopted, by which friends of
members, who are accepted as communicants in their own Churches,
may be accepted to partake of communion. This was passed by Annual
Conference and recommended to the Churches in 1956.

[2] Recently a threefold Lectionary of Prophecy, Epistle and Gospel
has been recommended to the Churches.

[3] See Acts ii. 42 ; Justin Martyr, 1 Apology, lxvii.

element of praise. The whole Church being a priestly body, it is its duty and privilege to offer *spiritual sacrifices*. We come not only to receive grace from God, but to *offer* worship to Him through the merits of our Lord's sacrifice, which at this service we plead. And so this service is an offering by the royal priesthood of worship, the fruits of our lips, of ourselves, our bodies, souls, and substance, which is a reasonable and lively sacrifice. This is acceptable through His intercession and sacrifice upon which we spiritually feed. This worship has been carried on with strict simplicity. There has been an attempt to combine simplicity with reality. There has not always been complete success; the ideal has not always been reached. Sometimes, as in other Churches, a lack of due reverence may have crept in; but it is by no means countenanced, and we can claim that simplicity and reverence of a very deep and satisfying kind may go hand in hand.[1]

So far as the doctrine of the Lord's Supper is concerned, Consubstantiation and Transubstantiation have of course been repudiated as metaphysical explanations of the Presence in the Lord's Supper, which are most misleading and altogether opposed to the teaching of the New Testament; but the merely memorial aspect

[1] The exigencies which have compelled us to use Churches for other purposes than those of worship, such as Sunday Schools, have played a part here. But there is a manifest desire to-day for buildings more congenial to the spirit of worship—buildings which may be reserved for its sole purpose.

has been repudiated.[1] Whilst then there has been a total lack of superstition attached to the service, there has been a definite emphasis on the Spiritual Presence associated with the Communion.[2]

Without elaborate ritual, then, and without vestments, Churches of Christ have found very satisfying, this worship centring in the Lord's Supper, conducted with dignity, simplicity, and quiet reverence, witnessing to the bond of fellowship which unites the members of the " beloved community " to one another and to their Divine Head, and which joins the Church on earth to the Church in heaven. Here in the Lord's Supper they have found a sure, yet silent witness to the Presence of the Lord, when in the fellowship company they have experienced the communion of the Body and Blood of Christ.

---

[1] The hymns which have been written for the Feast all show this clearly. One of the best known in the current Hymn Book is by Mr. G. Y. Tickle :

O what a feast ineffable is this !
    Thy table spread with more than angels' food —
Angels the highest never taste the bliss,
    The dear communion of Thy flesh and blood.

The formularies officially presented to Geneva declare the object o the Lord's Supper to be :
  (a) A memorial feast showing forth the death, resurrection, and expected return of the Christ.
  (b) A spiritual communion of the Body and Blood of the Lord to those who worthily partake.

[2] See *Scheme of Redemption*, p. 429. Mr. David King wrote in 1854, " The intelligent believer receives the bread and fruit of the vine *as such*, but at the same time *constituted* to him the body and blood of his now risen Lord, so *associated* that to look on them is to re-behold his Saviour's death."

CHAPTER XI

THE GREAT DOCTRINES

WITH regard to the great doctrines of Christianity
—the doctrines of God, of the Person of Christ,
and of the Atonement—there is need to say
little ; for it is not here that Churches of Christ
have made their greatest contribution to religious
thought. They differ in no sense from orthodox
Christianity in these matters, except that they
have always protested against making metaphysical explanations and theories of these
doctrines *binding upon the consciences* of Christians.
They have always declared that the Christian
Faith is centred rather in *facts* than in theories
about facts, and have protested that these great
dogmas about God and Christ are best spoken
of in the chaste language of the New Testament.[1] But this refusal to use the specula-
tive language of the creeds and confessions has
sometimes led to charges of unorthodoxy against
Churches of Christ. They have been said to hold
Arian, Sabellian, and Socinian views. Such
charges are *entirely unjust*, and arise out of a total
misunderstanding of their protest against the

[1] We rejoice to-day that modern theology is tending more and
more in this direction.

metaphysical language of the creeds and confessions.[1]

So far as the doctrine of God goes, Churches of Christ hold what is the normal Trinitarian view, though they have preferred not to use the terms Trinitarian, Unitarian, etc., as savouring too much of metaphysical explanations of the Godhead. But to describe their view as Unitarian, because they have preferred not to use the definite expression Trinitarian, is foolish. The Doxology has always been in constant use in Churches of Christ, and Baptism has always been administered into the Name of the Father, and of the Son, and of the Holy Spirit.[2] Moreover, the personality of the Holy Spirit has always been emphasised and the fact of His indwelling in the Church and the individual Christian stressed.

So far as the doctrine of the Person of Christ is concerned, Churches of Christ have ever accepted the fact of His essential Deity and His essential Manhood. It is true that Campbell, who wished to confine his terms to those actually used in the New Testament, disliked the expression, " eternal Son " and preferred, like the early Alexandrian school, to speak of the " eternal

[1] Note that Prof. Curtis, in his *Creeds and Confessions of Faith*, regards Churches of Christ as entirely orthodox on these matters (p. 307).

[2] The teaching of the early reformers on the Doctrine of God is most clearly expressed in an article by Campbell in the *Christian Messenger*, Vol. IX, pp. 317 ff. This article would convince the most astute critic that Campbell was orthodox.

Word."[1] In this he has been followed by Churches of Christ generally, but to say that, because of this, he accepted Adoptionism, or Arianism, regarding the Son as a created being though superior to all other created beings, is altogether to misunderstand him. Rather, all he was protesting, and what we are all ready to protest to-day, was, to use his own words, that " language fails and thought cannot reach the relation in which the Father and the Son have existed, now exist, and shall for ever exist." He declared that " there is, and was, and evermore will be, society in God Himself, a plurality as well as a unity in the Divine nature," and here he anticipated a very modern way of approaching the doctrine of the Godhead.

So far as the work of Jesus Christ, accomplished through the Incarnation and the Cross, is concerned, emphasis has always been placed on His redeeming work. But Churches of Christ have refused to make *theories* of the Atonement part of the Faith. The fact that Jesus died for our sins has been accepted by all, but no theories

---

[1] In this he was like Marcellus of Ancyra, though, unlike him, he did not regard the Incarnation as producing any change in the nature of the Diety. It would be interesting to discover whether Campbell was at all influenced by the celebrated Moses Stuart of Andover, whose teaching resembled that of Marcellus. See Foster's *History of New England Theology*, Chapter X. In writing against Arianism Campbell said, " The Scriptures nowhere teach me that the Son in His highest personal nature, had a beginning of being or existence ; '*the Word was in the beginning with God*,' even that Word ' which was made flesh and dwelt among us.' '*The Word was God*,' and as such I venerate ' the Word made flesh,' ' as God manifest in the flesh.' "

have been advanced.[1] There has been a remarkable sanity in the use of terms, and extreme revivalist hymns, many of them using language about the " blood of Jesus " which could not be justified from the New Testament, to say nothing of its being in bad taste, have generally been rejected. Here again, Churches of Christ have been misunderstood and accused of preaching a "water salvation," and of " substituting the water for the blood of Christ." Needless to say such charges are false, and due to misunderstanding. As we have seen in a previous chapter, Churches of Christ have placed great emphasis on Christians *following in the way of the Cross*, but this has not meant a denial of the substitutionary element in the life and death of Christ. But it has led to an idealism in life, to acts of self-denial, and to a high moral tone in general. There has been in the general body of the Churches a total lack of that sentimental and unctuous piety which sometimes characterises those who see only a substitutionary element in the Atonement, and there has been no room for the cult of perfect holiness ; for members of Churches of Christ have felt very keenly that we must " work out our own salvation with fear and trembling, for it is God who worketh in us " ; and have realised that He bore His cross that we might bear ours victoriously.

[1] Here we have a striking similarity to the course of history in the first four centuries of the Church ; for none of the three ancient creeds contains any theory of the Atonement, largely due to the fact that controversy in this period was centred solely in the doctrines of God and the Person of Christ.

Chapter XII

SOCIAL CHRISTIANITY

FROM the beginning of the Movement there was a recognition of social values. The emphasis which has always been placed on the Church and on *corporate salvation*, has kept Churches of Christ from any narrow individualism; and the doctrine of grace held from the beginning has kept back that stream of other-worldliness which has characterised some forms of evangelical Christianity. The pioneers recognised that man was a *social* animal, just as did Kingsley and Maurice in another sphere. It was said by Campbell that there were in the world three social institutions of divine appointment—the family, the Church, and the State. The supreme position given to the Church made these early reformers averse to setting up other societies outside the Church, such as Temperance societies, etc.; but this did not mean, as it has meant in some small bodies of Christians, that members of Churches were to neglect their duties to the State and to social reform as such. Rather, the opposite was stressed. Moreover, the absence of millenarian views has helped in this direction.

Members of Churches of Christ have always been interested in, and have been active supporters of every kind of social reform ; though they have refrained from *political*[1] action, and have always stood firm against any kind of political tradition in the Church which would make it a sort of understood thing that members should belong to one political party or another. That every member should recognise his duty to the State they have urged, but they have recognised that it is not the Church's duty to give *political* guidance, or to demand corporate action in any capacity which would limit the freedom of the members in political adhesion.

In every social and philanthropic work they have been ready to share as individuals, and as Churches. Especially has this been so in more recent times.[2] Mr. Sydney Black, of whom we have spoken, founded a social and philanthropic mission, to which is attached a Boys' and Girls' Orphanage. It is no exaggeration to say that this mission has done much to transform one area of Fulham from a slum into a respectable district. The late Mr. H. E. Tickle was one of Scotland's most ardent temperance reformers, and Chairman of the Scottish Permissive Bill Association. Both in Australia and America, orphanages are established in connection with the Churches.

[1] Throughout this chapter I use " political " in the sense of *party* politics.

[2] In this country, Australia, and America, members of Churches of Christ have taken their full share in local government, acting as magistrates, and sitting in the different state and national Houses of Legislature.

Sunday School and Temperance work have always been carried on vigorously, though the Churches would of course, quite rightly, resist the making of total abstinence a condition of Church membership. Both in America and in this country the Churches helped considerably in the anti-slavery campaign, and so unanimous was the policy in America that Disciples avoided any split over the matter. The Churches are always ready to help the work of hospitals, the Bible Society, etc., by taking up special collections ; and during the Great Wars they assisted considerably in war relief and in the protection of refugees. They have vigorously opposed war in all its forms, though again, as in the case of total abstinence, they have refused to make pacifism a condition of Church membership. The Churches in this country were represented on the Copec Conference, and some of the American Disciples were amongst the prominent members of the Stockholm Conference. They have in this country, through their Annual Conference, constantly petitioned Parliament on such matters as war, armaments, gambling, temperance reform, and the preservation of the Lord's Day, and their interest in social questions is witnessed to by the existence of a standing committee on the subject, and by discussions connected with it at conventions and conferences. Yet they have always seen clearly that social Christianity is not the whole of Christianity, and especially to-day are alive to the value of that spiritual communion with God which is so essential to all true religion.

These things are not written by way of boasting, but simply that readers may know what is the genius in Churches of Christ on these matters. We are all conscious enough of lamentable failure at this very point—failure to realise, even in a small measure, the passion for *social* righteousness which filled the heart of our Divine Lord.

It is only necessary now to refer to some special features which characterise Churches of Christ in general, so far as this country is concerned.

(1) They have never countenanced pew rents or appropriation of seats. They have ever urged that God's house should be a house of prayer, and open to all who wish to enter it, without money or price.

(2) They have believed in carrying on their work by the free-will offerings of the members. Consequently there are no collections in their public services, unless for charitable purposes. The only normal service in which an offering is taken is at the celebration of the Lord's Supper, and then the offering is part of the worship of the Church. Bazaars, and similar efforts of doubtful wisdom for the raising of funds, are not generally approved.

(3) They have refused to make class distinctions within the Church. All members are brethren wherever they meet, and it is no exaggeration to say that amongst them there is a remarkable display of real brotherhood.

(4) So strong has been this sense of brotherhood, that the Church has acted as a benefit society, granting relief to necessitous cases. Of course, as the State has gradually taken over some of these duties, the obligation on the Church has become less; but in necessitous cases such relief is still granted from Church funds. In this the Churches have followed the example of the New Testament Churches.

Chapter XIII

CONCLUSION

AND now that our task is ended, we are conscious that we have not written a *simple* statement of what Churches of Christ stand for. This we might have done in a certain way, and it would have covered no more than a few pages. But as Mr. Selwyn has recently said, " simplicity of definition is not necessarily an advantage, except for the more superficial kinds of appeal."[1] Having no desire to make a *superficial kind of appeal*, and knowing full well that such appeal, if desired, could be better made by other means, we have essayed the more difficult task of an historical survey of the Movement, convinced that in this we shall make our appeal to those who are prepared to *think*, and to think deeply, on the things of the spirit.

But in a few words we may briefly sum up those vital elements of truth to which Churches of Christ have witnessed. Throughout the history of the Movement, as in all movements, there have been elements of weakness and strength. But throughout there have never been lacking those signs of vitality, of growth,

[1] *The Approach to Christianity*, p. 241.

and of vision which are essential to all movements whose future holds any prospect of success. With regard to the whole development of modern thought—the contributions of science and philosophy to theology, the historical method of Bible study, the quickening of the social conscience—Churches of Christ have had the same experiences as most sections of the modern Church. But progress has been steady and the future is promising.

Of elements of weakness we may note two. Zeal for the Faith once for all delivered to the saints, here and there, may have appeared to be a little intolerant. But such intolerance — a thing which is apt to manifest itself whenever there is deep conviction, as there should always be in religious matters—is not, nor has it been, characteristic of the Movement ; nor should Churches of Christ be judged by it wherever it is manifested ; for their only desire is that men everywhere should exercise that freedom of judgment which God has given them, and seek the truth as it is in Jesus Christ. A second element of weakness has undoubtedly manifested itself in the *conduct of worship*. Especially has this been marked in the middle period of the history of the Movement. Whilst the essentials of true Christian worship have been maintained on a theoretical basis, sufficient attention has not been given, in the past, to the actual conduct of worship, and the development of the devotional spirit. In the past the whole matter was perhaps conceived on far too rigid a basis, with the consequent shrinking of the spiritual element, and in many places there was a total lack of regard for those elements of beauty which minister so richly to the needs of the spirit. But a better day has dawned, both here and in America. Articles are constantly being written on this subject, and conventions are concerned to discuss it. There is an increasing effort to impart dignity to the services, as well as *beauty* and *reality* too.

What, then, are the positive contributions of this Movement, whose growth numerically has been so rapid and shows no signs of abating ?

(1) In the first place, it has borne unflinching testimony to the value of the New Testament as the sacred record by which all Christianity must be judged, and it has insisted on the *historic method* of interpretation. (2) But at the same time it has insisted on the Divine character of the Church, visible on earth ; and the central position within its life of the two great sacraments of Baptism and the Lord's Supper. Moreover, as to these sacraments, it has maintained that they must be interpreted not only *spiritually*, but *ethically;* that is, that they must result in a new life devoted to the will of God. And so it has stood throughout its history for purity and righteousness of Christian life, and has fostered self-sacrifice, zeal, and devotion. (3) It has witnessed to the *centrality of Christ* in Christian discipleship, and so has stressed the

conscious yielding of the whole man—intellect, emotions, and will—to Him in loyalty and trust, as the test of discipleship. It has therefore rejected that early departure from this vital principle of Christianity, which sanctions the administration of Baptism—the badge of discipleship—to unconscious infants, who cannot exercise choice, being incapable of either belief or repentance. But whilst it has practised Believer's Baptism (immersion), it has never lost sight of that high doctrine of Baptism which is found in the writings of Paul, and which has been held by the Church since its foundation in Jerusalem. (4) It has also witnessed to the spiritual satisfaction which comes from weekly corporate worship centring in the Lord's Supper. (5) By its aversion to creeds and confessions, it has shown how to combine a maximum of liberty with a sane order and orthodoxy, and how to show a united front with a minimum of ecclesiastical organisation. (6) And finally, it has witnessed, with an undying passion, to the need for a real organic unity of Christ's Church. This is the historic task of Churches of Christ. They have never ceased in their " earnest efforts to promote both by testimony and practical labours the unity of the people of God." Nor will they cease until " we all attain unto the unity of the faith, and of the knowledge of the Son of God, unto a full-grown man, unto the measure of the stature of the fulness of Christ."

APPENDIX A

ANSWERS SUBMITTED TO QUESTIONNAIRES
SENT OUT BY THE SUBJECTS COMMITTEE
OF THE WORLD CONFERENCE ON FAITH
AND ORDER: 1920-5

I.—The Ministry

1.—What degree of unity in the matter of order will be necessary in the reunited Church?

A sufficient degree to represent the Church's spiritual unity. As seen in the New Testament this will include the recognition of a ministry, and provision for the due observance of Baptism (the immersion of penitent believers) and the Lord's Supper. In the ordering of Christian worship, the Lord's Supper will need to be restored as the central act of worship on the Lord's Day.

2.—Is it necessary that there should be a common ministry universally recognised?

Yes.

3.—If so, of what orders or kinds of ministers will this ministry consist?

Of Elders (Presbyter-Bishops), and Deacons in each local Church, together with a wider ministry of Evangelists or Missionaries, outside the local Church.

4.—Will the reunited Church require as necessary any conditions precedent to ordination, or any particular manner of ordination?

Yes, both.

5.—If so, what conditions precedent to ordination, and what manner of ordination ought to be required?

The conditions precedent to ordination should include: (*a*) A definite consciousness of a Divine vocation to serve; (*b*) a definite choice by the body with whom the ministry is to be exercised; (*c*) tests of faith and character; (*d*) ability to fulfil the duties of the Office.

In the case of Elders and Deacons very definite qualifications are found in 1 Timothy and Titus, and these should be required.

The manner of ordination should be by prayer and the laying on of hands.

II.—THE CHURCH

1.—How was the Church founded? Is it in any specific sense a Divine institution?

The Church is a specifically Divine institution, founded by our Lord through His Apostles, who were its first rulers and legislators. It rests, therefore, not on the will of man but upon the creative will of God. It is the high function of the Church to administer the revealed will of the Lord, and as His Body to carry on His work on earth, obeying in all things His behests, who is the Head.

2.—What are the essential characteristics of the Church, and in particular what is the relation of the Church to Christ and to the Holy Spirit?

As there is but one Christ so there can be but one Church, and this Church has its expression in this world in visible form. As a visible Church it consists of those who are being redeemed by Christ. This visible Church as instituted by Christ should manifest itself as a fellowship of men and women united with Him and with each other. It stands as His witness on earth and is set for the spread of His Kingdom.

The Church is the Body of Christ and He lives in the Church, and in its members, through the Holy Spirit. The Church is thus the temple for the habitation of God through His Spirit, and the bodies of individual members are temples of the Holy Spirit.

3.—What are the Visible marks of the Church on earth ?

The visible marks of the Church should include : (*a*) The profession of a definite faith in God as revealed in Jesus Christ who was the pre-existent Son of God, " God manifest in the flesh," and who was made both Lord and Christ. (*b*) The observance of Baptism and the Lord's Supper, the former the mode of admission into the membership of the Church, and the latter the central act of the Church's worship each Lord's Day. (*c*) A ministry as outlined in answers to the first questionnaire. (*d*) An ideal of Christian life, protected by disciplinary powers vested in the Church. (*e*) Freedom from financial support from those outside its membership.

4.—What is the relation of the Church to the Churches ?

The relation of the Church to the Churches is as described in the New Testament, a relationship in which the local Church is the representative of the One Church. The situation which at present exists of denominational Churches, existing together in the same locality, is not in accordance with the mind of Christ nor the organisation of the early Church.

5.—What is the relation of the Church to the Kingdom of God ?

In the New Testament the Church comes to occupy the position of the Kingdom of God, spoken of in the Synoptic Gospels. In a very real sense then the Church can be spoken of as the Kingdom of God, and yet in another sense the Kingdom is wider than the Church.

III. THE SACRAMENTS

PART I : The Two Rites which all Christians call Sacraments

1.—Should the United Church insist that all persons must be baptised before they can become members of the Church of God ?

Yes. In the New Testament Baptism was into Christ, unto the remission of sins, and in order to membership in the Body of Christ.

2.—Is it agreed that Baptism must be with water, and in the name of the Father, and of the Son, and of the Holy Spirit ?

Yes. This is the " one baptism " of the Apostolic Church.

3.—May all other points about Baptism (*e.g.* who may baptise ?) be left to other authorities than the central authority of the Church ?

No. It will not be possible to leave all other points unsettled. If the Church is to be reunited, and remain united, the question of the *mode* of Baptism will have to receive attention. It is now generally admitted that *immersion* was the Baptism of the Apostolic Church, and that for centuries it remained the only Baptism, both in the Catholic Church and in the usage of heretical sects. Baptism by pouring was only allowed in extremity, and then its full validity was doubted as in the case of Novatian (*c.* 250). Immersion is the invariable custom of the eastern Church, and Constantinople recently pronounced judgment on Anglican Baptisms (as still generally administered by aspersion), which judgment stated that the Orthodox Church could not accept them, even under the principle of " economy." With regard to sprinkling, it is a late custom which seems to have originated with the Genevan Reformers. We believe it is essential for the unity of the Church that the true symbolism of Baptism (burial into the death of Christ and resurrection with Him in the likeness of His resurrection) should be restored.

With regard to the administrator of Baptism, it has always been admitted, even by the Roman Church, that "lay Baptism" is valid if the proper "matter" and "form" are attended to.

4.—(a) Will those who have hitherto disallowed Infant Baptism, be willing to be members of the United Church along with those who make a practice of baptising infants?
No. This does not seem to be possible.

(b) Are there any other difficulties about Infant Baptism? If so, what are they and can they be met?

It is now generally admitted by scholars of all schools, that Infant Baptism very gradually came into use towards the close of the second century, and that it only became widespread as a result of Augustine's teaching about "original guilt" (see Harnack, *History of Dogma;* Williston Walker, *Church History;* Dollinger, *The First Age of Christianity;* Heiler, *Der Catholizismus*). For three centuries the normal rule of the Church was that Baptism was preceded by *faith* and *repentance*, on the part of the baptised. Neither do we think that Infant Baptism can be supported as a legitimate development of Apostolic practice; for where the full New Testament doctrine of Baptism is associated with it, Infant Baptism is bound to result in magical and unethical views of the sacrament being entertained. Christianity is based upon *a personal and individual choice*, resulting in the following of Christ as Lord and Saviour. There is in the Apostolic teaching no separation between *conversion and regeneration*, such as Infant Baptism makes necessary. Further, Infant Baptism cannot consistently be practised apart from Infant Communion, and in the West, at least, this practice has never been seriously entertained.

In view of the facts:

(a) Loyalty to Apostolic Christianity;
(b) Loyalty to the root principle of Christian discipleship, *i.e.* personal following of our Lord;

(*c*) The general practice of the Catholic Church during three centuries;

(*d*) The existence to-day of some nine or ten million Christians, who do not regard Infant Baptism as valid;

it does not seem to us possible to reach anything like a United Church, until this question is considered and settled.

5.—Should the United Church insist on the Lord's Supper as obligatory on its members?

Yes, the Lord's Supper was the central act of Christian worship, and at first the only service of corporate worship which Christians held. All the Baptised communed regularly at the Lord's Table, unless under the ban of excommunication. The Lord's Supper should be restored to this central place in the worship of the United Church.

6.—What is necessary to the celebration of this Sacrament in regard to (*a*) its matter (bread and wine), (*b*) its form (the words to be used), and (*c*) the minister of the sacrament?

(*a*) Bread and wine are the necessary symbols, and these should normally be pure wheaten bread and the fruit of the vine.

(*b*) With regard to the " form," there should be a blessing of the Bread and the Wine, and this blessing should—as has been normal in the Church from earliest times—be included in a prayer of thanksgiving. Normally the Words of Institution should be recited, but whether these should form part of the Thanksgiving Prayer or be declaratory, does not seem to be a matter which can be decided.

(*c*) It would seem that from earliest times the Presbyter has been the normal minister of the Lord's Supper, and this would *normally* be the case in the United Church. But seeing that the Christian priesthood belongs to the whole Church, it could not be denied to any Christian, acting under proper authority, to officiate at the Lord's Table.

7.—Is the holding of any doctrine concerning the Sacrament of the Lord's Supper to be regarded as necessary to its due celebration, or its due reception, or is the intention to do what the Lord did and commanded to be done sufficient for either or both?

It should not be held that the holding of any doctrine concerning the Lord's Supper is necessary to its due celebration or reception; the intention to do what the Lord did and commanded to be done, should be held sufficient for both.

8.—If there be any doctrine concerning the Sacrament of the Lord's Supper which the United Church should regard as necessary to due celebration or due reception, what is that doctrine?

Although the holding of any view with regard to the doctrine or purpose of the Lord's Supper should not be held to invalidate its due celebration (and this also holds good in the case of Baptism, which when the proper " matter " and " form " have been received, is not re-administered to a Christian because at the time of his Baptism he held a " low " or inadequate view of the sacrament); yet the United Church would seek to teach what has been held from the beginning; that the Lord's Supper is:

(a) A Memorial Feast showing forth or declaring the Sacrificial Death of our Lord, in such a way that to look on the bread and wine is to re-behold the Saviour's Death.

(b) A Spiritual Communion of the Body and Blood of the Lord to all the Baptised, who with faith and true repentance receive.

(c) An offering by a royal priesthood (the whole Church) of Worship, the fruits of our lips; of ourselves, our bodies and our substance; which is acceptable only through the pleading of His sacrifice, upon which the royal priesthood spiritually feasts.

Part II. Rites which many but not all Christians call Sacraments

1. (*a*) Should the United Church hold it to be a matter of obligation for all baptised persons to receive Confirmation ?

(*b*) What are the essential parts of Confirmation and by whom should it be administered ?

(*c*) What steps between Baptism and admission to the full privileges of membership in the Church are taken in Churches where Confirmation is not practised, and do these steps involve principles of general obligation ?

(*a*) No. Baptism is the rite of admission into the Body of Christ.

(*c*) In the case of Baptism being administered only to believing penitents, Baptism itself admits to full privileges of membership. Very often the admission to membership in the local Church is corporately symbolised by the giving of " the right hand of fellowship " with appropriate words, accompanied by such acts as the whole congregation standing, and the singing of a doxology or blessing. This corporate recognition of membership takes place at the baptised's first Communion. Bui such a ceremony is not held to have the same validtty as Baptism. It does not, as Baptism does, effect membership in the body of Christ, and cannot therefore be held to be obligatory.

2.—What should the United Church hold, or allow to be held, about confession of sins and absolution of the penitent, both public and private ?

In the first place, it should be made perfectly clear that confession of sin, whether public or private, is to God alone, and He alone grants absolution. But it is clear that it is the Church's duty to exercise discipline, and this discipline will normally be exercised by the Church's officers—those who have the rule over the Church. In the case of serious and open sins against the whole body of the Church, excommunication may be necessary, followed by confession and re-instatement of the penitent. In the case of less serious sins a member of the Church may desire—and indeed find it necessary for his own peace of mind—to unburden his soul to some godly man and to seek his spiritual guidance as well as his prayers. Normally such godly men would be the Presbyters of the Church. Such unburdening, to have any value, must, however, be spontaneous and voluntary, and the spiritual director must be careful to point the soul to God, who, alone, in Christ Jesus, absolves us from our sins.

There will certainly be cases of discipline which it would not be wise to bring before the whole Church, and to treat in a public way. In such cases discipline will normally be administered by the Presbyters.

3.—Should the United Church have any common and obligatory laws about marriage, the promise to keep which will be a condition of the solemnisation of a marriage by the Church, and the breach of which will make offenders liable to excommunication ? If so, what laws ?

Yes. Marriage is a sacred institution for which our Lord legislated, and which Paul treats as analogous to the mystical union between Christ and His Church. It is not therefore a mere matter of State legislation. It is in the strictest sense a Divine institution. The Christian doctrine is, that it is binding on both parties as long as either lives, and divorce, *i.e.* separation with re-marriage, would seem to be prohibited both by the teaching of our Lord and of Paul. The marriage vow is also one of chastity within the marriage bond, and both fornication and adultery carry with them excommunication—of course with the possibility of reinstatement of the penitent. Moreover, Christian marriage —like all Christian relationships—is based on the great principle of love (in the New Testament sense of the word). This differentiates it from other forms of marriage, such *e.g.* as Moslem and Hindu marriages.

4.—Should the United Church adopt any attitude as a body towards the unction of the sick ?

In the present state of discussion about this matter, it is hardly possible for the United Church to adopt any definite attitude, which would be binding on all. Such a matter as unction of the sick cannot be placed on the same level as Baptism and the Lord's Supper.

5.—Should the United Church regard, or refuse to regard, other rites than Baptism and the Lord's Supper, as Sacraments, or permit them to be so regarded by those who wish to do so ?

The question is really one of the meaning of a word· Many rites may be and are sacramental in the sense that spiritual grace is conveyed through material channels. In one sense the whole of life, for us, as creatures of time and space, body and spirit, is sacramental. Certainly there is a sense in which preaching, fasting, prayer, praise, the Lord's Day, confession of sins, are sacraments or ordinances. The main point will be to guard the centrality of Baptism and the Lord's Supper as the two great sacraments of Christ's institution, and to guard against the introduction of other rites, which have neither the sanction of our Lord nor of His Apostles.

APPENDIX B

BIBLIOGRAPHY

ANDERSON, JAMES. Outline of My Life. 1912.

BROWN, ALEXANDER. Conversion to God. 1887.

CAMPBELL, ALEXANDER. The Christian System. 1835. The Christian Baptist (7 vols., edited by). 1835.

COLVER, J. L. and WILLIAMSON, A. Training for Church Membership. 1940.

CURTIS, PROF. WILLIAM, D.D. Creeds and Confessions of Faith. 1911.

DAVIES, PROF. WITTON, D.D. Article in *Transactions of The Baptist Historical Society*, Vol. VII. 1921.

DAVIS, M. M., M.A. How the Disciples Began and Grew. 1915.

GARRISON, W. E., M.A., D.D. Alexander Campbell's Theology. 1900. Religion Follows the Frontier. 1931.

GORE, T. J., M.A. That They May All be One (edited by). 1909.

GRAY, JAMES, M.A. Discipleship in the Church, 1935. Dr. Whale and Infant Baptism, 1942.

JONES, WILLIAM, M.A. The Millenial Harbinger (2 vols., edited by). 1835, 1836.

KING, LOUISE. Memoirs of David King. 1897.

MASTON, A. B. Jubilee History of Churches of Christ in Australasia. 1903.

MCLEAN, ARCHIBALD. Collected Works (7 vols.). 1823.

MILLIGAN, R., D.D. The Scheme of Redemption, 1869.

OLIVER, LANCELOT. New Testament Christianity. 1911.

PHILLIPS, T. The Church of Christ. 1907.

RICHARDSON, ROBERT, M.D. Memoirs of A. Campbell (2 vols.). 1868.

ROTHERHAM, JOSEPH BRYANT. Let us Keep the Feast. 1910. Should Creeds be Mended or Ended? 1904.

TYLER, B. B., M.A. History of the Disciples of Christ. 1894. (Vol. XII. of *American Church History Series*.)

WALKER, DEAN E., M.A., D.D. Adventuring for Christian Unity, 1935.

Several Writers.—For His Name's Sake. 1921.

Harmsworth Universal Encyclopædia; articles *Campbell, Alexander*; and *Disciples of Christ*.

Encyclopædia Britannica; articles *Campbell, Alexander*; and *Disciples of Christ*.

Encyclopædia of Religion and Ethics; article *Disciples of Christ*.

THE END